HOME AT LAST

HOW TWO YOUNG WOMEN WITH PROFOUND INTELLECTUAL
AND MULTIPLE DISABILITIES ACHIEVED THEIR OWN HOME

of related interest

Listen to Me
Communicating the Needs of People with
Profound Intellectual and Multiple Disabilities
Pat Fitton
ISBN 1 85302 244 6

Young Adults with Special Needs
Assessment, Law and Practice – Caught in the Acts
John Friel
ISBN 1 85302 231 5

Community Care Practice and the Law
Michael Mandelstam with Belinda Schwehr
ISBN 1 85302 273 X

HOME AT LAST

HOW TWO YOUNG WOMEN WITH PROFOUND INTELLECTUAL AND MULTIPLE DISABILITIES ACHIEVED THEIR OWN HOME

Pat Fitton, Carol O'Brien and Jean Willson

Foreword by James Hogg

Jessica Kingsley Publishers
London and Bristol, Pennsylvania

The right of Pat Fitton, Carol O'Brien and Jean Willson to be identified as authors of this work has been asserted by them in accordance with the Copyright, Designs and Patents Act 1988.

First published in the United Kingdom in 1995 by
Jessica Kingsley Publishers Ltd
116 Pentonville Road
London N1 9JB, England
and
1900 Frost Road, Suite 101
Bristol, PA 19007, U S A

Library of Congress Cataloging in Publication Data

A CIP catalogue record for this book is available from the Library of Congress

British Library Cataloguing in Publication Data

A CIP catalogue record for this book is available from the British Library

ISBN 1-85302-254-3

Printed and Bound in Great Britain by
Biddles Ltd, Guildford and King's Lynn

CONTENTS

DEDICATION

Remembering Kathy's life and her struggle to live as she wished. For Victoria and Lisa, in support of their continuing enjoyment of their independence. For all the young men and women like them, who deserve to have the chance of a home of their own.

This book is intended as an inspiration to others.

ACKNOWLEDGEMENTS

This book has developed from a report of the same title about the Kendal House independent living project, originally commissioned by Pat Fitton and Jean Willson, written by Carol O'Brien, and funded by MENCAP City Foundation. Jessica Kingsley encouraged and guided us in moving from a basic narrative account to a practical guide for those considering similar projects. We are grateful to MENCAP City Foundation for a further grant towards expenses incurred in producing the final manuscript.

Professor James Hogg, Harry Marsh and Judy Wurr kindly read and commented on the manuscript, and their advice has been invaluable in shaping the final work.

Simon Palmour, the then Principal Officer for Learning Difficulties in the London Borough of Islington, inspired and encouraged the parents through all the difficulties in getting the project off the ground.

Carolyn White and Denise Hall, Kathy's and Victoria's social workers respectively, took up this project enthusiastically and their commitment contributed enormously to its realisation.

We want to thank the care agency and their support workers for the essential contribution they have made to increasing the independence and enriching the lifestyles of Kathy, Victoria and Lisa.

The friendship and experience of other families over the years have contributed to the improvements in services for which we have campaigned, and have supported us in continuing the struggle when we were weary. We wish to mention especially Marion Gabriel and her daughter Samantha, Pauline and Tony Davis, parents of Lisa, and Alyson and Bob Ruddick and their sons Perry and Adam.

We shall never forget Lynda Steele from the Spastics Society who encouraged and inspired us in our campaign to bring our children back to Islington to live in Field End House.

Andrew Wilkes, formerly of the London Borough of Islington, was much more than a social worker in his warm support of our endeavours in making a meaningful life for Kathy and Victoria. In a crisis he was always there, with support and practical solutions to seemingly insurmountable problems.

Barrie Fitton and Norman Willson have shared all the struggles outlined in this book, as partners and fathers. Without their support in the various campaigns and the back-up they unfailingly offered, often unobtrusively and behind the scenes, it is unlikely that the successes described in this book would have been achieved.

Finally we remember Kathy's joy in life, and the continuing determination of Victoria and Lisa to get the most out of life, against all the odds, and we see this independent living project as, above all, their achievement.

Foreword

People with profound learning and multiple disability offer society a number of significant challenges. The question as to whether they can benefit from education is surely answered by now, certainly for children, and increasingly in further education facilities for adults. Their ability to gain from social and leisure provision in the community has been amply demonstrated in a number of innovative projects across the United Kingdom. And examples of life in ordinary houses – both with family and staff – have increased during the past decade.

No one would wish to argue that the potential of people with multiple disabilities to participate in the community in these ways has been fully realised, however. Indeed, in some parts of the UK a view persists that a congregate residential setting staffed by nurses is an appropriate form of provision, with many people still languishing on the wards of long-stay hospitals or in large nursing homes.

Home at Last provides not only an antidote to such pessimism, but a practical demonstration and guide to how a home in the community can be established and run for adults with profound and multiple disabilities. The book is remarkable for achieving two, potentially incompatible, goals: first, it sets the development of Kathy's and Victoria's home in a small house in Islington against the background of two families' often harrowing experiences of dealing with statutory authorities in their bid to gain quality services for their daughters; second, the book sets out a clear strategy for establishing such a house and running it effectively. The development and costing of individual care packages, the evolution of an operational policy, service agreements, financial management and budgeting are all documented in detail, and provide a blueprint for similar initiatives.

While Victoria Willson continues to enjoy life in her own home, Katherine Sirockin shared this experience with her for only four months, tragically dying in August 1991. The significance of this bereavement is movingly described in the later chapters of the book, as are the process and principles of finding a new tenant with whom Victoria could share her life.

I have had the privilege not only of reading *Home at Last* in manuscript, but of visiting Victoria in her home. Aside from the pleasure of that morning, the visit also enabled me to confirm the reality described in the book. I hope it will be read by policy makers, service providers and parents alike. But I am sure that the authors' hope is not only that the book will be read, but that its contents will significantly influence provision for people with profound disabilities. Certainly no one reading the story of both parents and their daughters can be left in any doubt regarding the standards that have been set for all of us involved in this field.

Professor James Hogg
Director, the White Top Research Unit
University of Dundee

Introduction

You will meet Kathy and Victoria shortly in their individual chapters. You will then understand why the process of setting up an independent living project for them seemed at first so daunting, because of their profound intellectual and multiple disabilities, and why the authors felt the achievement in establishing it should be publicised.

For most young people, a vital element of growing up involves loosening parental ties and leaving home. The family will in most cases still be very important in their lives, but they will want to make their own way in the world in the manner and with the people they choose.

For young people with profound intellectual and multiple disabilities this stage in their development may never take place. Most stay at home well into adulthood, as parents feel the alternative forms of provision are not acceptable. Some parents are offered no alternative, and some may be reluctant to let go because their life has necessarily become so focused on the one they care for.

What are the usual options for residential provision?

LONG STAY HOSPITALS

Although there are fewer of these, there are plans for some to remain. Those remaining now tend to specialise in particular groups, such as those with severe challenging behaviour.

LOCAL AUTHORITY RESIDENTIAL UNITS

These have often not catered for people with profound and complex disabilities. Following the 1990 Community Care legislation, they will play an increasingly less central role as local authorities are obliged to purchase the vast majority of care packages from private or voluntary sources.

PRIVATE/VOLUNTARY HOMES

These have always formed a significant proportion of residential provision, in some cases specialising in more profound and complex disabilities. The Community Care legislation will ensure an increasingly important role for this sector.

INDEPENDENT LIVING SCHEMES

These provide support for people living either in their own or their family's home, or in rented accommodation. The care input is designed to meet the needs arising from the nature and extent of the disabilities. Such schemes have until recently usually been set up for those with less complex disabilities.

FOSTERING OR ADULT PLACEMENT SCHEMES

Individuals are placed with a family who will care for them as a member of the family on a long or short term basis. Such schemes can be very successful but do not as yet provide for large numbers nor generally for those with the most complex disabilities. To some extent the same considerations about leaving home will still apply as if this were the disabled person's own family.

When parents are seeking residential provision, what are they looking for?

- Good quality of care and a fulfilling lifestyle.

- Reliable monitoring of standards.

- Good communication with care/support staff.

- Continued participation in decisions relating to the welfare and lifestyle of the young person.

- Encouragement to continue their relationship taking account of the changes taking place as the young person matures, and as a result of the experience of leaving home.

Most parents worry about poor standards of care, even cruelty and abuse; difficulties in communication with the residential unit; distance and difficulties in travelling to visit or in having their son or daughter home to visit, and missing the person who until now had been so central in their lives.

If the person with profound intellectual and multiple disabilities lives long enough, the decision about leaving home will be forced as parents become more frail and eventually die. Local authorities do not generally plan for such contingencies, even though many will have hundreds of elderly parents caring for people with disabilities necessitating considerable support in their daily lives. Consequently, when parents become ill or die, hasty and ad hoc decisions may be made. These can result in inappropriate placements, far from the home community of the person with disabilities. Often, life with parents is replaced by life in an institution, however small scale. Real independence is not necessarily attained, and the transition to this would need more lengthy and careful planning than usually takes place in these circumstances.

Kathy and Victoria, the young women whose story this is, had experienced between them all the different forms of residential care. For much of the time their parents were not satisfied with the quality of care they were given. The parents felt their daughters' lifestyles could be further enriched, and they wanted them to achieve as much independence as possible. Above all, they wanted their daughters to be settled and secure in their living arrangements, so that as parents became incapacitated or died, they would not have to cope with fundamental upheavals in their arrangements as well as bereavement.

This book describes how the idea developed that Kathy and Victoria would have their own home, and that the twenty-four hour care they needed would come to them. Despite the profound and complex nature of their disabilities, their parents were determined that they would achieve their own home.

It was not an easy process; there were difficulties, some of them considerable, and some of these have not yet been resolved. However, the benefits for the young women involved have been so great that the authors felt the story should be told to inspire and help others planning residential arrangements for people with profound intellectual and multiple disabilities. We hope this story, with all the practical details of how to do things at various stages, and examples of the documentation essential to the project, will encourage parents, advocates, social workers and planners to think of more independent lifestyles for those with the most profound and complex disabilities.

This project was planned around the needs of Kathy and Victoria. Although Kathy was very frail when they both moved into Kendal House in April 1991, her death from pneumonia four months later came as a great shock to everyone involved with her. Eventually Lisa Davis took Kathy's place at Kendal House, in March 1992. You will find, therefore, that the story of the project and the accompanying documentation feature Kathy and Victoria, but that then Lisa appears in Chapter 6 as later stages of the project are described. This is explained at the end of Chapter 5, and the transitional period between Kathy's death and Lisa moving in is described fully in Chapter 8.

With the changes in assessment and provision coming about as a result of the 1990 Community Care legislation, we would hope that young people like Kathy, Victoria and Lisa will have all possible options examined for a fulfilling lifestyle. We hope this book will influence that process.

CHAPTER 1

KATHERINE SIROCKIN

At 27, Kathy was only four feet tall, but she impressed people with her personality and her enormous will-power. These qualities stood her in good stead all her life, enabling her to cope with the periodic crises which occurred due to her disabilities of cerebral palsy, rheumatoid arthritis, severe epilepsy and other chronic illnesses.

Kathy had a wicked and infectious laugh, and enjoyed going out to the pub, or to the theatre and concerts, and travelling. She also enjoyed splashing about in the swimming pool, and floating with armbands on. Eating was one of her favourite occupations, and she could feed herself, but needed help with all aspects of her personal care. Her diet was strictly controlled to reduce any exacerbation of her bowel inflammation. Her favourite foods were boiled eggs and smoked salmon.

She could not walk and used a special wheelchair to support her in a good sitting position. She communicated by pointing, directing her eyes and with some special sounds. She might cry if she needed something or disapproved of anything. When she was pleased she would smile and laugh, and clap her hands. To indicate a need, or to reject something being offered, she would point, lean her body, push or pull the person with her. She had a range of sounds which indicated her pleasure or unhappiness.

Kathy was born on the 17th November 1963. She had cerebral palsy and severe learning difficulties from birth, the causes of which were un-known. She screamed a lot in those early years, and started to walk only when aged four. At four and a half she developed severe rheumatoid arthritis, and was in a high fever for four months. All her limbs were seriously affected, becoming increasingly deformed as a result, and she never walked again. She continued with severe episodes for many years, and was probably never free from pain. After this initial attack, she was in and out of hospital for three years. Her developing speech and toilet training were all lost during this period.

At nine she had an operation on her left hip to remedy dislocation and infection. After this her hip remained fixed, making sitting more difficult, standing and walking impossible. At ten she began to have convulsions. By her mid twenties she suffered many different types of fit. At sixteen she developed severe inflammatory bowel disease, subsequently diagnosed as Crohns Disease, but rediagnosed in 1990 as collagenous colitis. At twenty she was given a permanent naso-gastric tube, which she continued to use for taking her drugs and for occasional fluid intake to avoid dehydration. At fourteen she started wearing splints on her wrists. The arthritis caused her wrists to drop, and would have eventually fused the joints. The splints ensured that the wrists would fuse in a useful position and not folded over.

When she was seven, she spent some time in Tadworth Hospital. Shortly after this, after much heart-searching, her parents told their social worker that they could no longer cope with caring for Kathy at home. The social worker put together a list of possible residential homes, and asked the parents to identify those that would be suitable. However, they quickly discovered that most places would not be prepared to accept Kathy, including those that claimed to provide for the most disabled. In the end there was no choice. The only place that was prepared to accept Kathy was The Beeches in Suffolk. The reason why they had been prepared to accept her soon became apparent, as her parents realised that the place was a disaster, badly run and a threat to Kathy's well-being. Following the death of another London girl the *Sunday Times* revealed that 43 children from The Beeches had died during the last twenty years. A Government Enquiry followed, and the Harvie Report recommended inspection of all residential children's homes. Because Kathy had not been in the care of a local authority there had been no official inspection or review of her care by an external agency, and for a long time no one had taken the parents' concerns seriously.

Kathy was only in the Beeches for ten months but her health deteriorated during this time, due to neglect and over-use of drugs. She had dysentery and bedsores that had not healed. Her parents took her to Great Ormond Street Hospital in London for treatment and she remained there for three months.

The *Sunday Times* highlighted issues of concern raised by events at The Beeches and, following the publication of several letters, a number of parents of children at The Beeches, including Kathy's parents, came together. Other parents then contacted them, and with the parents of the girl who died, and Marion Gabriel, a parent from Islington, they set up COMPASSION, the

Committee of Parents Against Sub-standard Subnormality Institutions and Nursing. Their aim was to promote better standards and more openness in institutions.

From Great Ormond Street Kathy was moved to Winifred House, which was an annexe of Harperbury Hospital in Hertfordshire. This was eventually taken over by Barnet Social Services Department, and Kathy subsequently moved into a ward in a long-stay hospital.

The ward had recently been modernised, though still obviously an institutional setting, and was divided into sleeping bays each with six beds. The thirty or so patients came under the enlightened regime of the consultant, who encouraged staff to treat them as individuals. However, the parents felt it was not good enough. They felt the care was regimented, and they hated to see the patients lined up in various stages of undress for toileting (or 'processing through the sluice' as it appeared to the parents) at set times. None of the patients had any personal possessions and when toys or clothing were taken in they always disappeared within the week. The television was on constantly, with the sound turned down, and the record-player provided continuous background noise. Many of the children spent their time lying on their beds pretending to be asleep, or banging their heads against the cot sides. If Kathy's parents visited when she was apparently asleep, they had only to whisper her name for her eyes to immediately open. Making any changes, for example, obtaining agreement for Kathy to wear trousers to keep her warm, was an uphill struggle. The attitude of the nurses was usually 'If you don't like it you can always take her home'. Any attempt to campaign for improvements made the nurses very defensive.

Kathy eventually left the hospital and came to live in the newly set up Field End House in 1978. When she was nineteen she moved into a residential unit in Hackney, returning to Islington in 1991 when she moved into a new respite care unit, before taking up her tenancy of 95 Kendal House.

Tragically, Kathy was only able to enjoy her new-found independence for four months, and even that was hindered by her increasing ill-health. She died in hospital on the 17th August 1991.

CHAPTER 2

Victoria Willson

Now 24, Victoria has a beautiful smile and a wry sense of humour. She always wears brightly coloured clothes, and enjoys good company, going for walks, and food. Her great passion in life is music, from Madonna to Mozart. She is a very positive person, clear about who and what she likes. She is very responsive to physical contact, and likes people to talk to her and interact with her. She likes flicking pieces of paper, especially the shiny crackly kind. She enjoys having lots of activity going on around her, and is quite happy to just sit and watch. She enjoys the bustle of city life – the traffic and crowds. She enjoys going swimming, splashing about and drinking the pool.

She communicates through facial expressions and with different sounds. She smiles when she is happy, and looks people in the eye. When she is not pleased, or she is bored, or wants something she moans and shouts, getting louder if there is no response. Sometimes she will reach out for something she wants or to be hugged.

In 1976, when Victoria was six years old, her mother, Jean, described her like this: 'A beautiful little girl with dark grey eyes, short auburn hair and a healthy tan sits on the floor with her head on one side listening intently to Vivaldi's Four Seasons… Her face is totally absorbed in the music and a smile hovers around her mouth and slowly widens into a contented grin from ear to ear. This is Victoria, my severely mentally and physically handicapped daughter, who is given to violent fits of rage that can smash and destroy most objects, and reduce an adult to a gibbering mass of nerves after a screaming attack that can last up to six hours or more.'

Victoria was born on the 26th June 1970. At the time her parents and four-year-old sister were living in a damp, rat-infested basement flat, rented from a private landlord in Islington. On New Year's Eve, before Victoria was born, her father remembers saying, 'Things can only get better!'. The flat was in a slum clearance area, and eventually a housing visitor called on the family. Having seen their circumstances, she promised them priority for rehousing. However, the months went by, and other families were moved from the street, their vacant houses boarded up. Soon only five families were left. The housing visitor returned, and her first question was, 'Haven't I seen you before?'. The papers had apparently gone missing. The family look back on that first occasion almost with a laugh, after a lifetime of dealing with inept officials, lost papers and inadequate excuses. Eventually the family was rehoused by the Council on a newly built estate.

When Victoria was born the doctors pronounced her normal. The family's happiness lasted barely three weeks, when she began having trembling limbs that soon rocketed into infantile spasms. She then spent several months in and out of hospital, while the doctors sought to diagnose her condition, and her family went through a living nightmare. At six months old she was diagnosed as having tuberous sclerosis.

When Victoria was three, they were allocated to a social worker. Victoria had screamed and cried for up to twelve hours a day since she was born. She rarely slept, and demanded constant attention from her mother. The whole family was suffering as a result; her sister was having problems with school and her father was working long hours. The social worker asked them how much longer they felt they could go on like that? The distraught answer was, 'Not for much longer,' and so the search began for somewhere where Victoria could live and be cared for.

The social worker arranged for Victoria's parents, Jean and Norman, to visit a number of places, including the long-stay mental handicap hospital for people from Islington. Jean remembers vividly the increasing horror and despair she felt as she was shown round the large, bleak wards. Eventually she turned to the consultant and said, 'I wouldn't leave my cat here'. He replied that it would improve, and that parents like Jean and Norman would be good for the hospital.

Eventually, the only establishment to offer Victoria a place was a voluntary home near Dorchester, 140 miles from her home. Jean and Norman found the staff there friendly and felt at the time that Victoria would be well cared for so, with anguish and many misgivings, they agreed to her moving there. Victoria was then aged four.

Jean and Norman continued to visit her regularly, and their misgivings grew. There were thirty children in the home, spending much of the day in a huge playroom which had few toys and a television, permanently on, behind a wire screen. Even today Jean feels a strong dislike for television. Then the ethos of the home changed. Staff were required to wear uniforms. Jean and Norman became increasingly concerned about the lack of therapy, and the over-reliance on drugs. Their concerns were not received sympathetically; the head of the home asked them what Victoria would need speech therapy for, since she did not speak.

However, around this time Jean and Norman did find a sympathetic and supportive forum in which to express their feelings and concerns, when they joined the parents' group Kith and Kids. They began to learn not to accept always what professionals told them was right for Victoria, but to fight for what they believed was in her best interests.

Although the voluntary home had accepted Victoria for life, they now proposed moving her to another house within the same organisation. In the meantime, however, the use of this house had changed, and it was no longer possible for her to go there. Jean and Norman were told that Victoria could only stay in the voluntary home for another two years, and then they would have to make alternative arrangements.

CHAPTER 3

Searching for the Right Patterns for Living 1976 to 1991

RETURN TO ISLINGTON

In 1976 Islington Council held a public meeting to consult with families of people with learning difficulties on its ten-year plan. Jean and Norman heard about it, and so did Pat and Barrie. So both sets of parents, who did not know each other, went to the Town Hall and listened carefully to the officers from the Social Services Department. Not a word was said about provision for people with severe learning disabilities, and when Jean asked a question, she was told that there were no plans. Leaving the meeting feeling angry and frustrated, they were stopped by a social worker with the local Spastics' Society, and over a drink in the nearby pub were joined by a few other parents with similar concerns. From this meeting the 'Families and Friends of the Mentally Handicapped in Islington' (FFMHI) was formed, with the intention of forcing Islington to bring their children back to the borough. They were encouraged to become a campaigning body, and given the confidence to do this.

Around this time an article in *Parents' Voice*, the magazine for parents produced by MENCAP, reported on a survey of councillors around the country. Out of fifty councillors interviewed, only three knew the difference between mental illness and mental handicap.

Against this background of ignorance, FFMHI began its campaign in Islington. To their surprise, parents discovered that there were councillors and officers who understood and were interested, and willing to take up their cause.

When the Government introduced joint financing schemes involving both health and local authorities, money became available to move people out of hospitals back to their home boroughs. It was proposed to use this funding to develop a residential home in Islington for the severely mentally handicapped children placed in homes a long way from Islington. Islington Council supported the proposal, but Islington Health Authority was reluctant to make a commitment. So FFMHI began a 'campaign of shame' which lasted for six months, including picketing meetings, issuing press releases and constantly lobbying, until finally the Health Authority gave its support to the proposal and agreed to fund its share of joint financing.

The parents had identified a building on the recently vacated site of the Royal Free Hospital in Liverpool Road. A project group was formed, including parents as well as representatives of the statutory agencies, and this met fortnightly in the old boardroom of the Royal Free Hospital.

It was agreed that the project would be based on a social rather than a medical model, and in this respect it was among the leaders in the field at this time. Members of the project group visited a number of places around the country, and Jean remembers being particularly impressed with Dr. Kushlick's methods in Henchard House, Dorchester, where the focus was on the individual needs of the children.

Islington Health Authority pulled out of the planning process at an early stage, but the Council was fully committed. The project team which carried out all the detailed planning work was a pioneering example of close co-operation between elected members, officers, other professionals, voluntary organisations and parents. That the new project opened only eighteen months later is evidence of the high level of commitment and sheer intensity of the work of the project team.

The new unit was named Field End House, a reference to the use of the site before Liverpool Road Hospital was built. It opened on 17th April 1978, and was formally opened a few weeks later by Barbara Castle MP, formerly Secretary of State for Social Services. Because the plans for the whole Royal Free Hospital site were still uncertain it was intended that a new location for Field End House would be found within two years. In the event, it remained there for ten years.

Field End House gave Jean and Norman the opportunity to participate again in the care of Victoria, and to contribute in a real way to her home. When Victoria returned to Islington, aged eight, she would not look at anyone. The lower part of her body was wasted because of the lack of physiotherapy. She woke every night, and it was thought that this may have been because night staff at the voluntary home had more time to pay her attention than did the day staff. Gradually her drugs were reduced, and she began to come out of her shell and to respond to her surroundings and the people in them. She also went to school for the first time in her life. From being a rather withdrawn pathetic, miserable child her parents watched her blossom into a much happier and more loveable little girl. In Jean's own words written at the time, 'No one will ever take away the gift of kissing my daughter goodnight again – that's what Field End House means to me'.

Kathy was fourteen when she moved into Field End House, and she lived there for five years. Pat and Barrie remember the excitement of the first months, of having her living so near, and the keenness of the new staff team. It was now so much easier to have her home for the weekend and holidays, and family relationships were re-built and strengthened.

This is, of course, no fairy story, and so it does not end here with a 'happy ever after'. Sadly, the sense of partnership and the enthusiasm were not sustained. After the initial excellent staff induction there was little further training or staff development. As staff left, they were not always replaced, speedily or at all. With the strain of staff shortages morale slumped, and the initial enthusiasm for a new project began to wear off. The service was not reviewed. The original vision of shared care never really came about.

It was, however, other external factors that brought about the closure of Field End House, by which time Kathy had moved out.

ON THE MOVE AGAIN

The Council had promised to plan and develop further accommodation for the young people in Field End House to move on to when they reached nineteen. But political power had shifted on the Council, and the new regime was very unsympathetic to parent participation and the development of local services. So when Kathy turned nineteen in 1982 the expected provision for young adults had not materialised, and there was nowhere in Islington for her to move on to. Nevertheless, pressure was applied to Pat and Barrie to find somewhere else for her.

At this time, they themselves were in the process of moving house, across the border into Hackney. They made contact with the local MENCAP, and learned of classes being held at the local Workers' Educational Association on different aspects of social issues, one of which would be on mental handicap. The tutor later told them he usually had about twenty people at these classes. But on the night Pat and Barrie went to hear him speak there were around two hundred people, crammed into the room and corridors at a local community centre. So much interest was generated that a follow-up meeting was arranged, and at this it was decided to set up Hackney Action for Mentally Handicapped People. They planned to campaign on several issues, but one of their earliest was about a property in Hackney which had been built for people with learning difficulties and then left empty for three years. Their campaign was successful, and in 1983 the unit opened and Kathy moved in.

Kathy settled down well into her new home, and was allocated a key worker whom Pat and Barrie describe as 'wonderful'. There was always a lot going on in the house, as well as trips out and holidays, and Kathy began to develop socially.

However, her bowel disease worsened, and in 1984 she went back into hospital for nine months. She had so much difficulty with swallowing that her parents, on her doctors' advice, took the decision that she should have a naso-gastric tube fitted permanently, to help with her medication and to ensure that she did not become dehydrated. They were then told that she could not return to the Hackney unit as she now needed nursing care. Great Ormond Street Hospital arranged for her to go to Tadworth Court, a respite and residential facility outside London, for a short while, and it was suggested that she could go back to the long-stay hospital. Her parents were determined not to lose everything she had gained, and argued strongly that she was being offered inappropriate placements because of her learning disability. They pointed out that if one of them required a naso-gastric tube they would not have to be cared for in hospital for the rest of their lives. Eventually, their social worker in Islington came up with a creative solution. He secured funding to employ workers from an agency funded by the Council to give care support to people with disabilities in their homes. They would work with Kathy every morning and evening, when she needed most attention. Kathy was now able to return to the Hackney unit.

Meanwhile, back in Islington, by 1987 the plans to demolish the Royal Free Hospital site were finalised, and Field End House was designated for closure. None of the replacement units was ready, however, and the parents were told it would be necessary for the residents to move into temporary accommodation for a period of three months. The seven young people still living in Field End House were rehoused in two vacant children's homes, one several miles outside Islington. Jean and Norman resisted the proposal to move Victoria out of the borough, because of their fears that she might never return. She therefore went to a recently vacated former children's home within the borough. This was not ideal for her, having inadequate facilities for wheelchair users. However, some of the children's home staff remained, and brought a refreshing new approach to Victoria's care.

Seven months later, the replacement units were still not ready, and the premises were needed to rehouse the children from another children's home, temporarily closing for building works. Victoria, her fellow residents and their staff were moved again, this time to a portakabin in the north of the Borough, originally designed for homeless families. It was a very unsuitable building, and staff morale plummeted. Jean and Norman took Victoria home with them every Saturday, otherwise she would not have gone out over the weekend. Staff left, and a new team came in.

The original plan for Victoria had been for her to move into a house with three other people, less disabled than herself. Shortage of money forced the Council to change these plans, and the new plan was that she would move, with the other young people from Field End House, to a purpose-built social services residential unit elsewhere in the borough. Little regard was paid to the individual needs of these young people, or to moving compatible people into a house together. However, in August 1990 Victoria did move there, and, despite her parents' misgivings about the arrangements, initially all seemed well.

However, as the months passed, Jean and Norman became concerned about the situation. They could see that many of the advances Victoria had made over the past year, due to the individual attention she had been given in the smaller group, were beginning to slip away. They themselves became very despondent, wondering indeed if all the battles to bring Victoria back to Islington had been worthwhile.

Nor were matters going well in Hackney for Kathy. The superintendant of her unit had left, and was not replaced for many months due to the Council's financial problems. There was no clear operational policy for the unit, and new staff received little training. Kathy's key worker left to study for her social work qualifications. Pat and Barrie frequently had no choice but to take Kathy home because sleeping-in staff had not been arranged or were not familiar with her care. She would spend the night with them, returning when they went to work.

By August 1989, according to Kathy's social worker, the situation at the Hackney unit had become frightening. There was a shortage of staff, and relations between Kathy's specially funded workers and the regular unit staff had deteriorated into personal conflicts, with arguments about who had ultimate responsibility for Kathy. Letters about the problems sent to Hackney Social Services by her parents and by Islington Social Services received no response.

There were problems with the other arrangements for Kathy as well. The taxi service which collected her from Hackney to take her to the day centre in Islington sometimes sent the wrong size car for her wheelchair, so that Kathy was unable to go.

The alternative solutions that were considered were to increase the number of hours that her additional workers would give to Kathy in the Hackney unit, or to move Kathy out altogether, possibly into one of the new Islington houses. Because of the legislation under which Kathy's original placement at Field End House was made, Islington remained responsible for funding her care, in the borough or out of it. A short term stay at Islington's new respite house was eventually agreed, provided that long term alternative arrangements were made.

THE IDEA OF INDEPENDENT LIVING

It was a conversation Jean had with a colleague that helped to sow the seed of the idea of independent living. Her colleague was unhappy with a social worker's inability to see the advantages for a man with learning difficulties of being supported in his own home, rather than moving to an institution. Suddenly this struck a chord with Jean and she saw that there might be other possibilities for Victoria.

Jean and Norman had continued their friendship with Pat and Barrie, and together they shared their fears and problems, as well as their hopes for the future. Slowly, the idea grew between them that instead of fitting Victoria and Kathy into whatever institution might be persuaded to take them, they could be cared for in an ordinary house, with arrangements made to suit them. Casual discussions became serious plans, and soon they had set to work on a new campaign, which seemed a more daunting challenge than anything they had previously undertaken.

To begin with, there was very little practical experience elsewhere of establishing individually tailored care in a community setting for people with a level of disability similar to that of Kathy and Victoria. Mainly because of the financial difficulties, due to the high cost of such care, most schemes provided support and care to groups of at least four people. In almost every case, the schemes pre-dated the residents, who were then assessed for their ability to fit into the scheme.

In neighbouring Camden, a similar project was being planned. This involved a group of parents of young people in their twenties and early thirties who were still living at home. These parents were working with professionals from the health authority, social services and the voluntary sector to set up a support service that would enable three of the young people to move into their own home. As the Islington and Camden parents all knew one another, a meeting was arranged to discuss some of the issues and to learn from the problems and successes that the Camden group had experienced in their planning. Later, when the Islington house was being developed, and before the two women moved in, the Camden parents were invited to visit it to see the practical arrangements.

The first hurdle to be overcome for Kathy and Victoria's parents was to secure the support of some key allies for the idea. A formal meeting was arranged with their social workers who became committed to the idea and pursued it energetically. Thus encouraged, the parents summoned up all their energy and determination to turn the idea into reality for their daughters.

The next hurdle was to find a suitable house or flat. They knew that in Islington this was not going to be easy. Relatively few properties were built or designed to wheelchair accessible standards, and the demand for those few was great.

The final hurdle was to find the money to fund the scheme. The first step was to identify potential sources of income and to draw up a realistic budget. Then this had to be 'sold' to the funders.

SETTING UP HOME TOGETHER

Following the meeting between the parents and the social workers, the idea was discussed with the Principal Officer for Learning Difficulties in Islington Social Services Department. At his request, formal memos were sent to him by the parents and social workers, requesting independent living schemes for Kathy and Victoria.

This officer had previously worked in services for people with physical disabilities in Islington, where the practice of setting up individual packages of care to support a person in his or her own home had been in operation since the mid 1970s. This practice had not previously been applied to services for people with learning disabilities. He saw the opportunity to adapt it to meet the needs of these two women, particularly because the parents were so committed to this approach, and they had the support of the care agency that was already working with Kathy. In a memo to the Assistant Director of Social Services in September 1989, the Principal Officer described the request for a special project as 'very significant'. In a further memo in October he set out more details of the proposed project, and pointed out that:

> 'The way forward for learning difficulty provision is individual packages of care. Whereas for physical disabilities this is common practice already, for learning disabilities it is new territory, but territory that will become the norm as we move from building-led services to need-led services. Given the commitment from parents and

care agency this is an ideal chance to blaze the trail to community provision.'

Following agreement from the Assistant Director to proceed to explore the feasibility of the proposed project, a meeting was arranged by the Principal Officer with both sets of parents and the social workers. A plan of action was worked out, which included identifying the women's care needs, finding suitable housing and obtaining the funding. This group continued to meet regularly as the project planning group with the addition of the manager of the care agency that had agreed to provide the support workers.

At the same time, in addition to the parents' pressure for alternative provision, the Social Services Department was being subjected to other pressures. Because of the deterioration in the Hackney service, which was already costing Islington a considerable amount of money, it was becoming increasingly obvious that other arrangements would have to be made for Kathy. No place could be identified in Islington, and Pat and Barrie were not prepared to accept a further place outside the borough.

Another pressure was that Victoria was one of seven people requiring a place at the proposed Islington residential facility, now agreed to be a six-bedded unit. Thus an alternative place for her would result in sufficient places for the remaining six people.

Following the first meeting of the project group, contact was made with two local housing associations, with a view either to finding an existing house or flat, or to exploring the possibility of constructing a purpose-built house on one of their sites. One possibility was the old Royal Free Hospital site, within which Field End House had been located, and which was now being redeveloped by one of the housing associations. At a meeting in November with Social Services, this housing association undertook to look for a suitable site.

An application was made by the parents to Islington Council on behalf of their daughters for tenancies in its own wheelchair-accessible stock, and for Council nominations to the housing associations.

The specification for the housing was drawn up by the project group. It included a wheelchair-accessible flat or house anywhere in Islington, but in a non-hilly area if possible, consisting of three bedrooms (so each of the women could have her own room plus a room for a sleeping-in carer), large living room, large bathroom designed around the women's needs, washing machine and drier area, kitchen with adequate room for wheelchair circulation and storage space. Also desirable was a garden and parking space. The flat had to be sound-proofed and double-glazed.

The parents also wrote to the Chair of the Housing Committee seeking his support for the housing nomination. He wrote two memos to the Social Services Department requesting information about the project in October 1989, to which the Department responded with outline information in November.

In January 1990 the housing association offered a new three-bed house on the Liverpool Road site of the old Royal Free Hospital. This was visited by the parents, but was felt to be very cramped. The lift was not big enough to accommodate a helper as well as a wheelchair user, and the house was on three floors, thus involving considerable use of the lift. So the offer was felt to be unsuitable, and was turned down.

In March 1990 the parents obtained an offer from the Council of a three-bed purpose-built wheelchair-accessible bungalow at 95 Kendal House, on the Priory Green Estate. Both sets of parents visited the house and felt it was suitable. The dream was about to become bricks and mortar.

When the bungalow was offered in March 1990 only its shell was completed. It had been decided within the Housing Department to delay completion until tenants were allocated so that the kitchen and bathroom could be designed around their needs. At a meeting of the project group in March the lettings officer stated that the building work, including all adaptations, had to be completed by Easter weekend in three weeks' time, when the builders' contract would end. Although this deadline seemed impossibly tight, it fitted in with the momentum of the Project Group to move forward now as quickly as possible. However such a speedy response proved to be impracticable.

The designs for the rooms were produced by the architect, in consultation with the parents and the occupational therapist. Due to the existing work programme of the Occupational Therapy section it was not possible for these plans to be completed before July 1990. At this stage, the Council agreed to delay the completion date and to bear any additional costs resulting from this. Once the plans were finalised agreement then had to be obtained for the capital sum of £10,000 to carry out the work. This was given in December, and the work was carried out in January 1991.

It was agreed that the tenancy would be a joint one in the names of Victoria and Kathy, commencing on 25th February 1991. The parents signed the tenancy agreement on behalf of Kathy and Victoria. This was the solution proposed by the Housing Department who initially resisted allocating a tenancy to two people who could not realistically take responsibility for meeting the terms of the tenancy in the usual way.

Meanwhile, Kathy moved back to Islington into the new respite care unit in February 1991 and stayed there for two months. She was happy and well cared for there, until she and Victoria could move, at last, into their own home in April 1991.

CHAPTER 4

PAYING FOR THEIR NEW HOME

The approval given to the Principal Officer for Learning Difficulties to explore the feasibility of the project for the two women included the requirement that it should not cost the Council any additional revenue money.

Islington Council was already providing full-time care and housing for Victoria, and funding a place in a project run by the London Borough of Hackney for Kathy. The cost of Kathy's place plus the taxi fare to bring her to her day centre Monday to Friday plus additional care support came to £53,000 per annum.

The Assistant Director of Social Services estimated that finding an alternative place for Victoria and thus freeing up a place in her proposed Islington placement would generate funds of around £17,000 per annum for her support. This represented the Borough's estimate of the average cost of a place in a private or voluntary home outside the borough.

The care agency was asked to calculate the cost of providing support for the two women. This took into account their daily care needs based on an itemised list of day-to-day tasks, Kathy's day centre place, the fact that Victoria would be leaving school in July 1990 with little prospect of a day centre place, and the amount of time each woman spent with her family. Social Services then required the amount to be reduced to bring it into line with the budget for the project. Details of costings for the Care Package can be found in Appendix A. The figures were refined over several months, but were in the region of £50,000 for each woman.

The Principal Officer then sought authority to 'actually proceed to a formal proposal, and some affirmation that it is likely to be supported'. At the project group meeting in March he was able to confirm that this approval had been given.

It was agreed by the project group that an application on behalf of each woman would be made to the Independent Living Fund (ILF) to make up the difference between the actual cost of providing an adequate level of care and the amount the Council was prepared to contribute. The Independent Living Fund is an agency handling government funds to be allocated to people with disabilities for the costs of their personal and domestic care. Kathy and Victoria met the criteria for applicants. The arrangements have changed since then and the current situation is outlined briefly at the end of this chapter.

The application for Victoria was made in October 1989 by her social worker. The ILF visiting social worker met with Victoria and her Islington social worker in October, and indicated that a recommendation would be made to the Fund to meet a proportion of the cost, based on an assessment of her needs. In November a letter from the Fund stated that the application could not be dealt with until more definite arrangements for her care had been made.

An application to the ILF was made on behalf of Kathy by Pat, but in March 1990 she received a letter informing her that the Fund were unable to consider Kathy's application.

In April 1990 the Principal Officer wrote to the Director of the ILF seeking clarification on the discrepancy between the two responses to the two very similar applications. The Director replied that the discrepancy had arisen because the ILF social worker who visited Kathy had thought that the project was to be a halfway house provided in the grounds of an existing residential facility. Since the two women would be occupying their home as joint tenants the ILF Trustees were now satisfied that this would be a genuine independent living situation. However, he wrote, 'the Trustees have temporarily suspended action on all new applications as a result of the Fund's present budget problems. They are presently seeking to redefine their priorities and the applications from Victoria and Katherine will need to be looked at in the light of the Trustees' final decisions'.

In June 1990 the ILF wrote to Kathy's social worker informing her that they were arranging for a further visit to Kathy by their own social worker, and they would then be assessing the two women's needs together.

On 28 June the Principal Officer wrote to the ILF with an update on the project, informing them that the total cost would be over £100,000 per annum, and that the Council would be funding up to £56,000 per annum. He also re-affirmed that this would be an independent project, with the women being joint tenants and their parents acting as guarantors.

At the end of August the ILF wrote to both Kathy and Victoria informing them, 'that the Fund is able to contribute up to £353.05 per week towards the cost of the care that you will be employing'. This figure was calculated on the maximum amount allowable for London of £400 per week, less half of the Attendance Allowance (now Disability Living Allowance, Care Component) (£18.75) and less Severe Disability Premium (£28.20). This worked out at £18,358.60 per annum each, £36,717.20 *in toto* in 1991 figures.

This was accepted at the following meeting of the project group in November.

It had also been agreed by the project group that the running costs of the house – heating, lighting, water rates, telephone calls and so on – would be paid for from the two women's personal income. This income would be made up of Attendance Allowance, Severe Disability Allowance, Severe Disability Premium, Housing Benefit and Income Support. Their transport costs would be paid for from their Mobility Allowances (now Disabled Living Allowance, Mobility Component). They would both be entitled to exemption from paying the community charge. Detailed information on these benefits is given in Appendix D.

Applications for these allowances were made to the local Social Security Office in February 1991, but by the time Victoria and Kathy moved into the house, although agreed, they had still not all been paid.

By October 1990 the costings had been finalised and are set out in more detail in Appendix A. The final formal approvals were sought and obtained from the Chair of the Neighbourhood Services Committee. It was agreed that the Council would contribute £55,990 pa to the scheme, with the balance of £36,717 coming from the ILF.

A NOTE ON THE INDEPENDENT LIVING FUND

ILF payments to people who received them under the original arrangements are continued by way of the Independent Living (Extension) Fund. The original arrangements were discontinued in November 1992 and the Independent Living (1993) Fund was set up to replace them. The ILF information leaflet explains the new conditions, *all* of which must be met by applicants who must:

1. be at least 16 and under 66 years of age,

2. receive the highest rate of the Care Component of Disability Living Allowance,

3. be at risk of entering residential care (or currently be in residential care and wish to leave and live independently),

4. live alone or with people who cannot fully meet the care needs,

5. be on Income Support or have an income above Income Support level which is less than the cost of care needed,

6. have savings of less than £8,000.

In addition, the local authority must be providing or agree to provide at least £200 worth of services a week.

It is not certain that under these new arrangements the care input required at Kendal House could have been fully financed. The ILF contribution to meet the shortfall between actual costs and the amount Social Services was prepared to contribute would now probably fall below the required amount.

CHAPTER 5

SUPPORT AT HOME

The scheme was based on the individual needs of Kathy and Victoria, and so a separate package of care was worked out for each of them. Both women required 24-hour care, but Kathy attended a day centre four days a week, when she was well enough.

The care agency which had agreed to provide support for Kathy and Victoria had considerable experience in managing support for people with physical disabilities in their own homes. From this experience they felt it vital to define clearly the relationship between the service user and their support worker. The support worker is seen as being there to enable the user to do what (s)he wishes. The user has to be able to direct the worker, and the worker is not expected to make judgements about what would be 'best for the client' in terms of their lifestyle. This puts the support worker into the position of empowering the user, rather than providing care to a passive receiver. It is the key to giving people with disabilities their independence, and respecting their rights as citizens.

In the course of setting up the packages for Kathy and Victoria, however, some difficulties with this definition emerged. This was the first time that this agency had worked with people who could not direct their carers, and who were dependent on other people making judgements about what was in their best interests. These difficulties have not yet been fully resolved, although it is intended that the Operational Policy will provide the ground rules. In the meantime, it is the parents who act as representatives and care managers. There has been much discussion in the project group, and since, about the relative roles of parents, representatives/advocates and care managers. The Council will need to look at these management issues as part of their Care in the Community Policy. It cannot be assumed that the parents can take on these roles, as often seems to be the case now. This issue is discussed further in Chapters 9 and 10.

Some of the care agency support workers were already familiar with Kathy as they had worked with her in previous residential settings in Hackney and Islington. Working with Kathy in her own home would therefore be an extension of the work they were already doing. The package for Victoria was, however, quite new.

The workers in the house are helped considerably by the enormous amount of information put together by the parents over many years. This includes life books, giving each woman's life history, and care books setting out the practical details of their daily care. This information is lovingly presented in bound covers, with many photographs to illustrate the women in varying moods and situations. The parents also put together an information book on all the household equipment and general upkeep and maintenance in the house. Examples of these are given in Appendices E and F.

It was agreed by the project group that the parents would draw up the Operational Policy for the scheme in consultation with the manager of the care agency chosen to provide support. This can be found in Appendix B.

Further details of the Care Package will be found in Appendix A. Details of the organisational arrangements for the support workers are given at the beginning of Chapter 7.

After Kathy died, Victoria lived on her own for several months. However, in March 1992 another tenant moved in to share the bungalow at Kendal House with her. Lisa Davis lived with her parents not far from Jean and Norman. She had respite care at Field End House during the time that Victoria and Kathy were there. Her support needs are now being provided through the same care agency, paid for in the same way as Victoria's. The two women are learning to share their house, and their new independence. How this came about is described in Chapter 8.

CHAPTER 6

COMMUNITY INVOLVEMENT

NEIGHBOURS AND THE LOCAL COMMUNITY

'It's a gnome miss…' the parents were greeted by local children with these words on a cold bleak day when they visited the shell of 95 Kendal House, to have another look round, to make sure they were making the right decision. The children had taken over the small walled garden as their territory and it was the builders who had told them what the house was for.

The parents chatted with them and it turned out that the gnome was a home and that it was for disabled people. So, the local community already had some idea that it was going to be for people who were different.

Kathy and Victoria moved in quietly with no fuss, and certainly not with an 'official opening' by someone famous. The parents made sure they spoke to those who passed the bungalow daily, walking their dogs, collecting papers. They were friendly and interested in the set-up. The workers were advised to be friendly, but never to invite anyone into the house. Some people were extremely curious, and would stop and stare into the windows. Venetian blinds and lace curtains were soon acquired.

The parents worked very hard at making workers understand that this was a high crime area, with a drug dealing centre on the very next block. The bungalow must never be left unlocked, no washing or other things should be left in the garden, as it would quickly disappear. Washing did disappear off the line, so anti-climb paint was applied to fence, wall and roof. The parents made sure the local lads were told and could pass this information on to their network.

The caretaker was a key figure to befriend. As time went by, the shops and street market and people living on the estate became more familiar with Kathy and Victoria. Victoria is now always greeted warmly wherever she goes, as many people in the borough know her family and she is after all a fourth generation Islingtonian. This means a great deal to her family. After twenty years of moving from place to place, she now has roots and is Home at Last as part of her own community.

Of course some people still stare, as if Victoria and Lisa come from outer space, but this is because they are different, they have to use wheelchairs and sometimes behave a little differently.

Recently Victoria developed a new kind of fit which causes her to scream a great deal. This has concerned the neighbours, who asked about her, as sometimes it sounds as if she is in agony. Once they understood the problem they accepted the situation. When unusual things happen around the bungalow, the neighbours will tell the Neighbourhood Office. The parents encourage this, as it means they feel protective and the house has its own neighbourhood watch.

Both families have many connections throughout the borough and this helps with attitudes and questions about the women, and in sorting out problems quickly.

More work would need to be done with neighbours by families and representatives if tenants were moving into an unfamiliar neighbourhood.

FAMILY, FRIENDS AND NETWORKS

The women come from very loving close families, whose expectations for their daughters were extremely high. The families are determined that everyone should treat their daughters with respect and concern for their dignity.

For Victoria there have been times when her family were the only constant people in her life. Like everyone else the women look forward to seeing mum, dad, brothers, sisters and grandparents. They enjoy visiting their family home, which is within walking distance. Both recognise the streets and get excited when nearing the houses.

It has not always been easy to maintain these links, as initially the staff teams' interpretation of independence was that the links should not be so close. It was only through a long process of talking with everyone, often done when parents were visiting their daughters, that the staff realised that even though the women were not living with their parents the family links were still vitally important.

Over the years the families' friends have become the women's friends. Willing and generous to raise money for furniture and other things for the house, they organised sponsored events, fun evenings and made amazing donations so that goods and money to around the value of £10,000 were eventually raised.

Certain friends in both families have become especially close and will take responsibility for a watching brief, for example when parents go abroad on holiday. They have also become guardians and trustees for them.

It is clear that without the families' involvement both Victoria's and Lisa's networks would be sparse. The parents recognize this and are trying to address it. But it has never been easy. Victoria belongs to Kith and Kids and over the years has had many volunteers who wished to become friends. A transient staff team who may be uncomfortable about input from an 'outsider' may unwittingly freeze out a potential volunteer. Victoria has two constant friends, Martha and Maria, who visit her when they can.

For people with multiple disabilities which include communication difficulties it is essential that part of their personal development plans should include action to foster friendships and volunteers, and to join groups that may enable them to widen their circles. Continued effort by workers is needed to maintain those networks that exist as in any normal relationship – sending cards and letters, organising and attending special occasions, making phone calls, and visits.

FINDING A GP

For people with multiple disabilities and complex medical needs, it is absolutely vital to be registered with a GP. To have a GP who is also sympathetic, listens well, has patience and sensitivity, and can learn from carers, and the women, would be a bonus.

It is crucial for these women because of their disabilities – epilepsy, scoliosis, tuberous sclerosis, Rett's syndrome, and learning disabilities. As there is no speech, often the women can appear in pain, generally unhappy or screaming in agony, but with no clear indication of the site of the pain. It is vital that physical checks are done as a matter of course, to eliminate the obvious and ease their pain.

There are, sadly, some people who deny that people with learning disabilities can experience pain. Continuing education and training therefore has to take place with workers to foster awareness so that they can identify when pain is present. For example, a pale face, dark rings under the eyes and general lethargy could mean a bad period pain or headache; administering a painkiller could alleviate this pain or discomfort.

A GP will be expected to provide a good baseline for someone so that their general health and wellbeing is maintained; diagnose and manage things such as chest infections; problem solve in situations such as allergies and skin breakdowns; monitor drug levels; and provide medication and supplies, which must never be allowed to run out.

When Victoria and Kathy lived in Field End House, a doctor from a local group practice used to visit. The parents approached the same doctor. Everyone was extremely relieved, when 95 Kendal House was set up, that he agreed that his practice should take on the women. Kathy was registered at the same practice but when she was at home with her parents her former GP would still see her if there were urgent worries.

When the women were registered, the GP was invited round to the house to meet them, before there were any particular concerns. This gave him the opportunity to meet them on their home ground when they were more relaxed, and it gave the parents and workers the opportunity to talk to him about them as people, and not just a set of medical problems. Also, the parents were able to give him written information about their respective conditions.

This preliminary contact was useful, as the next time he met them they may well have been very distressed with some problem that was not a straightforward matter to diagnose.

The practice has been efficient and welcoming to the women although their waiting rooms are small and disabled access is not good. When the surgery is full it is uncomfortable for the other patients if Victoria becomes too loud or too demonstrative.

PARAMEDICAL SUPPORT AND SETTING UP SYSTEMS

It is also vital to have access to a whole range of paramedics such as physiotherapists and occupational therapists who can give valuable support in ways of dealing with problems, supplying equipment and keeping the women in good health. Paramedical support is not always easy to acquire for people with learning disabilities; there can be problems with access and transport to facilities, and these resources are chronically understaffed.

Occupational Therapists (OTs) gave practical advice and resources when the house was being converted for Kathy and Victoria. The bathroom, shower and toilets were built to their specification after consultation with the parents. They have since helped with suitable seating and tailor-made bath chairs for both women. It is the OT who should help with the individual provision for the daily life care. Unfortunately, difficulties in communication between the care agency and the Community Team for People with Learning Disabilities have resulted in this not happening for some time, and Lisa and Victoria are not always receiving adequate provision.

Physiotherapists can only give minimum time due to shortages in the borough, but their input is still absolutely essential to maintain both women's mobility and prevent further complications. Over time systems have been established for the physiotherapists to monitor both women's exercises, to train and refresh all support workers, to advise on such items as lifting and handling, equipment and aids. They are involved in problem solving with body braces, calipers, boots, walking frames, hoists, seating and of course, the wheelchair.

The Community Nurses provides a service that workers can occasionally use, but in general only if there is a medical need such as dressings or injections.

The Continence Service is absolutely essential. If the workers follow the recording method, then re-ordering supplies can be maintained efficiently. It is often the little things that can slip. Plastic night sheets and net knickers seem always difficult to acquire. A little difficulty they had was disposal of used pads. As this is an ordinary house, waste is taken away weekly by the borough's Cleansing Department. Parents discovered the most hygienic and practical method of disposing of used pads was buying bulk orders of small strong plastic bags from the local butcher!

Dentistry is another important service. Finding a dentist sufficiently sensitive and willing to take the women on took time, but eventually a health centre was found. Both women really enjoy the experience. Good maintenance of dental hygiene is really important and should be part of a regular daily routine, which should include cleaning their teeth twice a day, and always inspecting their mouths for anything unusual. This prevents possible build up of larger problems such as abscesses or gum problems. Keeping their teeth in good condition is essential for chewing and speech development.

The Chiropodist visits the women in the house on a regular basis – again an experience enjoyed by both. It is important for people with feet problems to have regular checks to prevent difficulties escalating. A chiropodist can help with advice on circulation, footwear, management of hard skin and blisters, and aids for problems like crossed toes.

The parents learned how vital it is to identify what the women needed in the first instance from these paramedics, and then create a process and system within the house so that workers could easily follow instructions enabling the women to receive the service, and appointments to be made and kept. Maintaining communication with the team around these issues can be problematic; no one person is responsible and then the onus falls on the parents to co-ordinate services.

The bureaucracy and, at times, sheer incompetence that surrounds access to services often defeats people working with Lisa and Victoria. The parents must always be assertive, patient, tenacious and be prepared to take up complaints formally. All these measures have to be taken when, for example, anything goes wrong with the wheelchair. Due to a 'computer fault' one wheelchair order languished in a store room for four months, and when it did arrive had the wrong wheels, cushions, inserts, feet adaptations, and no belt.

THE SOCIAL WORKER

As part of the service agreement between the Borough and the care agency a named social worker must be allocated to ensure good practice. Unfortunately, the social workers allocated have only lasted a brief time, and for many months Victoria has had to use the duty system. In an area like Islington, turnover seems high anyway, and this was a period of re-structuring that involved the movement of some social workers. The Neighbourhood Office is an extremely busy one that deals with all the problems that inner city life can bring to families. Many social work posts are vacant in this office.

The previous social workers played a vital part in the planning and preparation of the move to the house; they arranged welfare benefits, housing benefits, community fund applications, and sorted out housing difficulties; followed up minor repairs, as well as making a valuable input into the overall planning of the project.

There is a vital need to monitor the service for Lisa and Victoria who, as individuals living virtually independently in the community, without their parents and family, are highly vulnerable. Their care package has never been without difficulties and the social worker should be the key person bringing all the relevant people together so that issues can be addressed.

DAY SERVICES

Before Victoria left school, it was quite clear that there would be no day service offered to her by the borough as there was already a waiting list of twenty-eight people, all with high dependency needs, waiting for a place in the Special Needs section of the Social Learning Centre (formerly Adult Training Centre). The prospect of no future formal day care provision was another reason to press for a home of their own where at least they would have a one-to-one staff ratio.

In the first year it became apparent that even a one-to-one ratio was not always enough for Victoria. Kathy did attend a day centre when her health permitted, usually four days a week. After Kathy's death, when Victoria was alone in the house, she became isolated, and also bored with the same people, For some members of her team, working with her alone on long shifts became difficult, and they left. Over a period of time she was adversely affected by the lack of opportunities for mixing with any groups of people except when she went to the cinema or a cafe, and then she was on the fringe.

Eventually, after much campaigning by the local MENCAP society, the borough did provide a small service for those people who did not have day care. The Flexi Team is a small group of workers, one of whom is assigned as a key worker to an individual, They are supposed to provide a tailor-made service to meet individual need. This is done on a one-to-one basis or meeting together in a small group. However, this service is rationed to a limited number of hours per week per person. The other disadvantages are that they do not have a permanent base, any means of transport or a transport budget. A changing team and staff shortages often make the service irregular.

However, over a period of time via the parent's grapevine, a good source of daytime adult education classes for people with special needs was discovered. For most days now, both Lisa and Victoria attend a class a day – wheelchair dancing, pottery, Let's make Music. The limitations on this are that they can attend any classes as long as they fit in with the staff's shift. No transport is provided and access is only available if a worker attends with the student. This means that not everyone without day services is able to attend.

Day services should complement daily living arrangements. For people with disabilities they provide continuing education, a change of scene, different people, new interests and a framework for the day. After all, unlike other people they do not have any alternatives for filling their day.

ACCESS TO SERVICES AND CLUBS

Often the fact that Victoria and Lisa have a combination of physical and learning disabilities, communication difficulties, and use wheelchairs means that they do not enjoy equal opportunities with other young women. For example, they do not have access to further education or the world of work. Sadly, this is even more apparent in their own learning disabled community, where they cannot attend the local branch of MENCAP's Beacon Club. It is felt that extra workers would be needed, and the club does not have appropriate transport for them. The club does accept their right to be there, but the practical difficulties prevent this. As a result of this all the club's outside activities – summer schemes, weekends away, trips to places of interest are also not available to them.

Inadequate physical access to many places, even in an enlightened borough such as Islington, with its many dropped pavements, and wheelchair access to most official buildings, is still a barrier for both women. One awkward step can make entry to some buildings impossible.

Many discos would welcome the young women, and their young workers have made many valiant attempts, but have often been daunted by the flights of stairs leading to the discos or by the unsuitability of the toilet's situation and layout.

Both attend a community-run club in an old laundry in the middle of an estate, which is exclusively for people with learning disabilities and additional disabilities. They both enjoy this club.

LEISURE ACTIVITIES

The women love company and respond well to places where lots of things are happening and the atmosphere is exciting. Fortunately, the bungalow is placed right in the centre of a vibrant housing estate, with lots of coming and going. Often just sitting at their lounge window or in the garden, watching their neighbours, or going to the local shops is very entertaining for the women. Being centrally located and within walking distance of Kings Cross and Euston stations has provided many leisure hours for both women and their enablers, and 'people watching' has become an art form. The local high street with excellent fashion shops, and even better a wonderful variety of cosmopolitan places to eat, especially al fresco, also provides leisure activities; the local antique market and street market are frequent visiting places.

There is a local swimming pool, just fifteen minutes away, which they both enjoy very much. They also enjoy going to pubs, tapas and wine bars, the favourite in the summer being the Waterside Inn by the canal. The canal lies adjacent to the house, and gives many hours of pleasure on calm walks along the towpath. Sometimes this calm is interrupted by Victoria testing the echoing effect of the bridges over the towpath. Her resounding yells cause consternation to fishermen, ducks and passing dogs. There are plenty of parks and the Georgian squares, with iron railings for feeling, provide daily outings.

Victoria and Kathy loved going to theatres and concerts. Belonging to SHAPE, an organisation which promotes access to the arts for people with disabilities, and getting excellent front seats, often boxes at reduced prices, encouraged their workers to plan their leisure time. Of course, sometimes the public reacted when either one become over enthusiastic with her audience participation, and more than once Victoria has been offered free drinks from the bar when a particularly quiet piece of music was about to be performed.

Loud colourful performances are enjoyed such as Joseph and the Technicolour Dream Coat and Circus Archaos. Anything that features the Muppets is a favourite of Lisa, and Mozart is a passion of Victoria. Once at the Coliseum, in a box just twenty feet from the stage, Victoria was having a gentle moan, flicking her usual paper; unfortunately she could be heard on stage. She was asked to leave, but was invited back for dress rehearsals.

Museums can also be a favourite pastime, not so much for content but for tactile experience, acoustics and people watching. The British and London Museums are best for the tourist watch.

Through their many outings, other people are being made aware that these young women have an amazing ability to enjoy music and theatre, and they are gradually being accepted in all walks of life.

TRANSPORT

One of the biggest single difficulties for a person with a disability is transport. For these women, who will never be able to use local public transport, the process of transporting them from A to B has been, and is, a nightmare at times. To ensure that either of them is in the right place at the right time for, say, a hospital appointment, means planning on the scale of a military operation.

They both have use of the Dial-a-Ride service, but this is heavily booked, may only be used by booking 24 hours in advance, and cannot be used for hospital appointments. The Borough subsidises a taxi card service, but only for 50 journeys per year. With no day care, these are used very quickly within a short space of time.

Limited to places within walking distance, dependent on the vagaries of the weather, the women were in danger of leading a very limited lifestyle, and of resulting social isolation.

So when Lisa had been in the house for over a year, the parents decided that their daughters' life style had become so limited without their own vehicle that they helped to buy one for them. It took some time and a lot of effort to acquire an adapted Volkswagen bus. Both women, with careful budgeting, and using their Disability Living Allowance mobility component, seem to be able to afford it. Lisa's father does all repairs, which is a huge saving. It soon became apparent that having at least six different people driving the vehicle creates its own problems. They do not see it as the women's vehicle; care is not always taken about parking, or reporting minor faults, and a simple problem such as a nut coming loose and not being dealt with at the time can mean hundreds of pounds of repairs.

But the advantages to the women and their workers are boundless. They are now able to plan holidays, weekends away and spontaneous trips such as walks over Hampstead Heath, looking at Christmas lights or can just go for a spin in their very own vehicle. The most important thing of all is that they can now attend their day classes, which provides the framework of their day.

SHOPPING AND MARKETS

The aims and philosophy of the house, from the beginning, were founded on encouragement of as much independence as possible and the belief that both disabled women should participate in the daily running of their home. Buying their own food and household goods themselves has been an important part of their weekly routine.

The bungalow is near a corner shop, for the odd urgent supplies. The street market and accompanying shops which include Sainsburys and Marks and Spencer are within walking distance and serve all their shopping needs. But, as with many things, manoeuvering and managing the wheelchair often calls for planning. For example, the route to the main shops leads uphill. Depending on how strong the worker is and if the wheelchairs are in good order, then the direct route may be taken. If the worker is not feeling energetic or the weather is windy, then a flatter, more circuitous route will be chosen.

Once at the shopping centre, timing must be carefully considered, as Victoria can be unexpectedly interested in people and things about her, which may mean she grabs at people and their bags in a crowd. It is better to choose a less busy time to shop. Some shops have, by their own planning or lack of good planning, excluded people with wheelchairs as their check-outs are too narrow or have steps leading in. The return journey is downhill, and with a wheelchair loaded with shopping this can be hard work and hazardous.

To maintain this essential mobility, great care must be taken by the team of workers to ensure that the wheelchairs are kept in good order. This is not always done, and when a wheel comes off, that woman is then trapped in her home unable to do her own shopping.

Although often seen as arduous and complicated, nevertheless it is a vital part of the women's lives and, by doing this every few days, their community presence has been established successfully and many people including stall holders know them by name.

Comprehensive systems have been set up in the House Book and Care Books for the workers to follow. For example, diets for both women are clearly laid out, in personal diaries and on the house's notice board there are spaces for every team member to add to the day's shopping list. The House Diary should include re-ordering of medication, library books to return, and the staff hand-over should include all relevant matters which might include shopping for the day. Workers need to exercise common sense and regularly check things like store cupboards, as no system is fail-safe.

LOCAL NEIGHBOURHOOD SERVICES

The parents had difficulties from the start with the Council services. The first indication, in the week when Kathy and Victoria moved in, was when the parents were constantly asking for the steel grilles to be removed from the windows. These are always put on empty property to prevent squatters, but become a huge fire risk once people have moved in. After one week the parents removed them, making sure the Neighbourhood Office knew that they were ready for collection. The local Neighbourhood Office is an extremely busy one, and has not had much experience of disabled people living in the community. This has caused a great deal of frustration and anger to their parents who have had to be very articulate and persistent in order to acquire and maintain good services for their daughters.

Initially, parents expected the staff team to carry out the essential checking that is part of the day-to-day running of the house, After a while it became evident that this was not being done reliably. A classic example occurred when one of the toilets began to leak from the bottom of its base. The amount of water itself was not great, and the repair at that stage was minor. Many visits to the Office were made by Victoria and her worker to report the fault, without success. The parents then took up the responsibility and started writing letters to the Estate Manager, Neighbourhood Officer, Housing Chairman and finally requested help from the women's ward councillor. Eventually, the repairs were completed but, because nine months had elapsed, the minor repair escalated into something major as Victoria eventually rocked the pedestal completely off the base; the flooring had to be replaced, along with tiles as damp had caused rotting. A worker injured her back as a consequence.

The emergency services – heating, gas and electricity – have been very efficient, once they knew that two very disabled women were tenants. Lisa and Victoria are still waiting for a disabled sign in front of the house's parking bays. The delay is caused by a dispute about which section of the Council's budget will pay for it.

The issue for parents is deciding who actually follows things through. Although the Operational Policy clearly outlines the duties, and the House Book sets out in great detail everything about running the house, no one person is ultimately responsible. In reality this means that things can remain not checked or left from week to week. If there are agency workers or new staff, the proper action may not be taken because, although these written directions are there and may be clear, they are not always read or followed.

VULNERABILITY AND SECURITY

The families are rooted in Islington, so know very well the nature and feel of the borough and especially the area where the bungalow is situated. The vast estate has a partially transient population; some flats are for elderly people, and one particular block is a focus for drug dealing.

The parents have been quite explicit in telling workers that they must be aware that the women live in a high crime area, and people have to be vigilant and take steps at all times to maintain the security of the house. For example, curtains must be drawn, all windows shut and locked before they go out; the steel chain and padlock must be placed in front of the vehicles; washing must not be left on the washing umbrella when they go out. Workers on the late shift are always taken home in recommended mini cabs.

Although parents continue to work hard to let workers know that they have to be continually aware and careful, nevertheless it is essential for them not to become nervous. Alongside this, involvement with the women's near neighbours and caretaker is encouraged. Parents have welcomed their watching and reporting, and they do. Many people have a certain protective feel about Victoria and Lisa. It is they who will telephone the police when they see people on the roof of the house, or something that looks suspicious, Parents have encouraged police presence, not only for security but also for education and involvement with the women.

However, parents have been very clear that the involvement with others is on the house's terms and a fine balance has to be maintained between a friendly watch and total involvement.

SEXUAL AND EMOTIONAL ISSUES

Although these issues are clearly identified in the Operational Policy, it is only slowly that the women's sexual and emotional needs are becoming apparent, and the issues that are being identified are not always addressed.

It is important that the people who work with the women are sensitive to their development of sexual awareness, whilst not making unfounded assumptions. It is also important that they receive on-going training in this area. Both sets of parents are now convinced that they do not want a male member of staff on the team. But both women enjoy the company of men, so the workers must ensure that this is done outside, via pubs and clubs. Personal invitations from the women to men to visit them in their own home then becomes their choice. It is absolutely essential to be aware of their vulnerability to abuse.

Daily personal contacts are made in many places, and at many levels. Both women look for affection and, in their own way, are able to return this. People working with them should be sensitive to their expressions of such feelings and respond to them with respect, treating them with dignity and offering them choices. In addition they should note any possible sexual attraction and discuss the development of any other caring relationship they observe to be developing, and share their observations and clarify issues with the women and their representatives.

CHAPTER 7

WEEKS IN THE LIFE OF...

The following accounts give a picture of life for the tenants at Kendal House during typical weeks.

The account of Kathy's week is based on diary records early in the project.

Victoria's week is based on more recent events, after Lisa took Kathy's place in March 1992.

HOW THE SUPPORT WORKERS ARE ORGANISED

This information on how support workers are organised will clarify the references to them in the following accounts.

Originally the workers were assigned to separate teams, one of three staff for Kathy, and one of four staff for Victoria; Victoria's team included the sleep-over allocation. The aim is still for assigned workers to work principally with one particular woman, but experience has led to some changes in the way this is organised. Factors such as staffing changes and sickness can mean temporary changes in the basic arrangements.

There is at the time of writing a team of seven support workers, as follows:

> Four full-time,
> Three part-time.

Lisa's workers do the following hours:

> On weekdays
>> 8.00 a.m. to 4.30 p.m.
>> 4.30 p.m. to 10 p.m.
>
> On Saturdays
>> 9.00 a.m. to 10.00 p.m.

On Sundays
    4.00 p.m. to 10.00 p.m.

Victoria's workers do the following hours:

    4.00 p.m. to 11 p.m. plus sleep-over,

then the same worker goes on from

    8.00 a.m. to 4.30 p.m.
    i.e. a 24-hour shift.

There is a half-hour overlap between shifts for a handover from one worker to the next.

When the project began, the care agency did not feel a co-ordinating post was necessary at support worker level. This position was revised in the light of experience and initially a team leader was appointed from within and for each group of workers principally working with each woman. Because of staff changes, at the time of writing one team leader is performing this co-ordinating role for all seven workers.

Whenever possible, support workers cover for one another in the event of sickness, holidays or unforeseen circumstances. When this is not possible, workers are employed from one commercial agency, and the pool from which they are drawn is kept as small as possible. However, inevitably at times a worker will be sent who has not met Lisa or Victoria before, and is not familiar with their needs. During their first shift they are therefore heavily reliant on the advice of the other worker and the information communication systems in the house.

It is interesting that in recent months, three of the commercial agency workers have joined the permanent staff team after initially getting to know Victoria and Lisa through covering for regular support workers.

Few if any of the support workers on the project have any formal training or qualifications in this area of work. The previous work experience of support workers has included residential work with people with physical disabilities, catering, youth work, work in a day centre for people with learning disabilities and home caring with elderly people. Some are working part-time at Kendal House while studying for higher educational qualifications or training in an unrelated field.

Some have had no previous experience of working with people with profound intellectual and multiple disabilities before working at Kendal House. Others have worked on voluntary schemes such as holiday projects with people with disabilities, or have related experience in caring for people with other forms of special needs.

The age range of the team varies from time to time, and a conscious effort is needed to maintain a balance of age and experience; for instance, by trying to include those who have experience with their own children and possibly grandchildren, as well as younger people of around the same age as the Kendal House tenants.

A WEEK IN THE LIFE OF KATHY

MONDAY

Maureen goes to Kathy's bedroom at 7.30 am and finds her stirring. Maureen quietly prepares things and waits for Kathy to wake naturally; sometimes if she is woken from sleep it can cause her fits to start. Kathy eventually opens her eyes and smiles at Maureen, then begins making grumbling sounds. She has some flickering eye movements, signs of fit activity, but nothing more. First thing in the morning Kathy has usually had a large, loose bowel movement – she has copious and constant diarrhoea as a result of a rare bowel disease. Maureen removes her soiled pad and cleans her thoroughly, laying her on bed pads to give her a break from the close fitting pads. Kathy smiles and makes appreciative sounds as she is made comfortable. Maureen now props her up on her pillows and brings in her breakfast – always a soft boiled egg with a slice or two of bread or toast, and a drink of warm soya milk. Kathy needs a slow start in the morning and experience has shown that if she has breakfast in bed she is better able to cope with the routine of bathing later. This also gives her joints, stiff with rheumatoid arthritis, time to ease into movement and for the medication to take effect before she is required to make the many movements needed for bathing and dressing.

Kathy eats most of her egg and bread with enjoyment, but will not drink from the cup. Maureen gives Kathy her medication (anti-convulsants, steroids, anti-inflammatory drugs, immuno-suppressive drugs and pain relief for the arthritis and bowel disease, and vitamin supplements because of problems in fully absorbing food) and the soya milk, all through the naso-gastric tube which Kathy has had since the most serious episode of her bowel disease in 1984. On good days Kathy eats and sometimes drinks, but if not she must have fluids regularly by tube or she quickly becomes dehydrated. Support workers and her parents have all learned to do this, and to replace the tube when required.

Kathy has a rest to let the tube feed settle, and then Maureen takes her for a bath. Everything needed must be ready in the bathroom, as Kathy cannot be left alone in the bath even momentarily because of the dangers of fitting and because she is not strong enough now to sit up without support.

She splashes with pleasure and enjoys the warm water and the gentle soaping, but makes complaining sounds when her hair is washed.

Maureen helps Kathy to get dried and then back in her bedroom, creams her whole body, gently massaging the stiff joints and doing her physiotherapy exercises as she goes. Kathy has more flickering eye movements so Maureen lets her rest for a while.

Kathy helps to choose her clothes by pointing at one of two items offered, and admires herself when dressed, looking down at her jumper and trousers and stroking them, looking at Maureen to share her pleasure. She has to rest for a while now. Maureen puts on some early choral music, and Kathy sits in her matrix wheelchair, moulded to a comfortable and supportive shape. While she looks through some clothes catalogues Maureen strips the bed, wipes down the protective covers and puts pyjamas and bed linen into the washing machine after rinsing everything in the sluice.

Getting up takes Kathy two to three hours, depending on how well she is. This morning was a good morning. Rushing her just brings on fits, especially the serious flop-outs, when she can be unconscious for several hours.

Maureen checks Kathy's wheelchair bag as she is going to the day centre – spare pads, bibs, tissues, packed lunch, lunchtime medication, diary, copy of the doctor's letter and list of medication in case she has to go to casualty. The centre keeps a supply of rectal valium to use if Kathy has fits there, and a community nurse comes in at lunchtime to give Kathy her medication and a tube feed, as centre staff are not allowed to do this.

Kathy smiles when the transport arrives. She usually enjoys the ride and the change of surroundings. She meets her friend when she arrives at the centre, and he helps her off with her coat and sits in the canteen with her while she is offered a drink. Later she goes swimming which she greatly enjoys, wearing armbands and splashing. She does not eat her lunch on return and sleeps most of the afternoon, probably tired after all the activity.

Rena welcomes her off the bus back at Kendal House, and gets a bleary smile. She offers Kathy a drink but gives it by tube after Kathy refuses it. Kathy plays with her nesting baskets on the floor, and then enjoys watching Rena make supper in the kitchen. She tries hard to eat her supper herself, but only manages a little fish and mashed potatoes. Rena helps her to eat a little more, but then Kathy suddenly gets very tired. She has her drink by tube, with her medication.

After a rest in the lounge, Kathy livens up and she and Victoria enjoy listening to some Mozart together. Later Kathy enjoys a cuddle with Rena, and then sits sociably in her wheelchair when some friends of Victoria visit.

By 10.00 pm Kathy is yawning and dozing. Rena takes her to wash and clean her teeth, then settles her into bed, changing her pad. Then she drinks a little of her camomile tea, and Rena gives her the rest by tube with her medication. She is then not disturbed even if she needs changing, for at least an hour. We have found by experience that especially at night, if Kathy is moved soon after tube feeding this can precipitate one of her floppy fits which can leave her vomiting, unconscious, cold, with low blood pressure and all the signs of severe shock. Tonight she settles to sleep quietly, with medieval music playing and cuddling her favourite pink doll. Rena is sleeping in tonight, and before she goes to bed herself she checks the intercom is working, and gives Kathy a last pad change to make her comfortable for the night.

TUESDAY

Rena is woken by hearing Kathy crying at 6.30 am. She goes into her room and finds Kathy very uncomfortable, having had a huge loose bowel movement. She talks quietly to Kathy while she cleans her and makes her comfortable on bed pads. She offers her a drink but although Kathy is calmer and has given Rena a smile of appreciation, she is still unsettled. Rena leaves her to see if she will drop off to sleep again and Kathy does doze; however, she is crying for attention again within half an hour. Rena finds she needs cleaning up again and then gets her breakfast. Kathy is interested but seems to have difficulty in actually eating. Rena notices that she is having occasional jerks in her limbs as well as frequent flickering eye movements, and this fit activity is probably making it hard for her to concentrate. Kathy manages a small amount of her egg and bread with help, and then has another massive bowel movement. Rena decides to split the medication and soya tube feed to lessen the strain on Kathy's digestion, and she gives her a rest of forty-five minutes in between each feed. Kathy dozes, and is not very responsive except to wake and grumble now and again.

She is quiet in the bath and does not show her usual enjoyment. The flickering eye movements increase and Rena finishes washing her quickly and takes her back to her room. She gives the physio a miss because of the fit activity, and creams and dresses Kathy slowly, taking her to lie down on the lounge sofa while she cleans the bed and puts the washing on.

Kathy dozes and by the time the centre bus comes she is a better colour and the fit activity seems to have settled, so it is decided she can go.

She sleeps on the bus but livens up when her friend meets her and goes with her to the cookery class. Kathy likes to watch the other students preparing food, and her friend helps her to mix up the ingredients for a cake.

She is interested to watch the finished product come out of the oven, but will not eat any, or touch her packed lunch. (Kathy has a strict dairy free, low fat and low fibre diet, which prevents her pain, discomfort and diarrhoea from being even worse, and everyone who cares for her in any setting needs to know what she is allowed, especially on occasions such as parties.)

During the afternoon Kathy goes out shopping with a small group of students from the centre. Usually she enjoys the busy high road, but today centre staff note she dozes, and is irritable when she wakes.

She sleeps in the bus home and wants to lie quietly in the lounge, listening to music while Lynette prepares supper. Lynette has to help Kathy to eat this evening, and it is a struggle to get her to take even a small amount. Later Kathy makes it clear that she wants to rest in her own room and not in the lounge, and Lynette spends the rest of the evening with her there, playing favourite music tapes and offering Kathy various of her favourite things to handle.

Kathy has several bouts of diarrhoea later in the evening and needs another bath, which exhausts her. She drifts off to sleep before Lynette has finished her night time fluids and medication, which she splits to try to avoid provoking more diarrhoea.

Lynette makes a note in the diary that Kathy is not as well as usual, and talks briefly to Jenny who is doing the sleep-in about checking her before she herself goes to bed. Jenny needs to clean and change her around midnight, but Kathy does not stir.

WEDNESDAY

Jenny checks Kathy when she wakes at 6.45 am and cleans and changes her, but Kathy hardly stirs. Maureen comes in to take over Kathy's care and has a quick look at the diary after Jenny has briefly handed over. She brings in breakfast but has great difficulty in rousing Kathy. She eventually wakes and manages some food, but gives up trying to feed herself and puts the spoon in the bowl. Maureen helps her to eat a little more, and notices Kathy is shaky. She gives her the medication and soya drink in two stages, and decides to give her a bed bath to avoid too much stimulation. Kathy enjoys this and the gentle massage with moisturiser, but Jenny decides not to try the physio.

Kathy seems a little more lively when she goes in the lounge and manages to inch herself off the sofa to drag herself over to reach some favourite objects. When the transport arrives Jenny decides she is well enough to go, although she mentions the earlier shakiness to the escort.

Kathy has the giggles when she arrives at the centre, and is very pleased when she finds today is her favourite music session. Her teacher manages to find a way of involving each member of the class in making some music during the session, and Kathy shows her appreciation by clapping and making joyful sounds. She goes to sleep afterwards and stays asleep through lunch time. Her friend sits with her and stays with her during the afternoon when she wakes and seems very irritable. She has some of her own things which are kept at the centre for tactile work, but shows little interest in these today and eventually throws some of them at her friend when he persists in offering them.

She grumbles on the journey home and Rena finds it hard to interest her in anything. She manages to eat a little supper by herself but when she has had enough pushes the bowl away so hard that it smashes on the floor. Kathy finds this amusing for a short while and Rena tries hard not to react, just clearing up without comment.

Later Rena and Jenny suggest to Kathy and her friend Victoria that they go out to the pub. At first the two young women enjoy eating crisps and the general lively atmosphere. However Kathy becomes irritable when offered a drink and eventually that goes flying. She gets more cross and Victoria catches the mood – Rena and Jenny decide it is time to go home.

Rena takes Kathy to her room and after a change and with some favourite music she seems more settled. Her diarrhoea is still very frequent, but eventually she is settled enough to drop off to sleep after her nighttime fluids and medication.

THURSDAY

Rena goes in to check Kathy at 7.30 am and as she is changing her, Kathy goes into a grand mal convulsion. Rena turns her over to the recovery position and times the fit at one and a half minutes. Kathy is comatose for ten minutes or so and then becomes restless. She has two further convulsions of slightly less than a minute, and Rena decides to give her 5 mg of rectal valium according to the care book guidelines. As often happens Kathy has a massive bowel movement after this and two further short convulsions. Rena gives her another 5 mg and sits quietly with her; she can go up to a total of 20 mg before medical advice should be sought if convulsions continue. Kathy has a few jerks of the limbs but eventually goes off into a peaceful sleep. Rena asks Victoria's worker to come in and sit with Kathy while she telephones the care agency to explain that Kathy will not be able to go into the centre today, and staffing will be needed during the day time. Fortunately, Rena is able to stay on, so she telephones the transport in time to cancel; they will let the centre know that Kathy will not be coming in today.

Kathy sleeps until mid-morning. As she seems calmer Rena gives her a bath, which she badly needs. She listens quietly to music in the lounge, and enjoys a cuddle with Rena. She is not interested in lunch so Rena makes sure she has a food supplement through the tube. During the afternoon she dozes and wakes to show she is enjoying the music. Lynette has taken over and at 4.00 pm she hears Kathy gagging, and turns round to find her having another grand mal convulsion. Kathy goes blue and finds it hard to get her breath; eventually it comes back with a great gasp. She has two more and Lynette decides to give her 5 mg more rectal valium. Kathy goes into a deep sleep, and will not be roused even for supper. She has food supplements by tube during the evening and is really completely out of it. Lynette makes careful notes in the diary for tomorrow's shift, and spends some time briefing the agency worker who will be doing the sleep-in tonight. Kathy's fit activity seems to have settled by 10.00 pm and she sleeps peacefully through her night time fluids and medication.

FRIDAY

Kathy is still asleep at 8.00 am even after two changes. There is no hurry today as she does not attend the centre on Fridays, so Maureen puts on a quiet Purcell tape and moves around getting things ready, talking to Kathy about what they might do today. Eventually Kathy stirs and Maureen gives her another clean and change. Kathy is quiet and still obviously tired, but she smiles to see her breakfast and manages to eat most of it slowly, even managing to drink some of her soya. Maureen gives her the rest of the soya and the medication by tube, and then changes her music tape to some more lively Renaissance dance music. After a rest Kathy is ready for her bath. She smiles at Maureen and makes happy sounds but is not as active as usual. Maureen does the physio exercises bit by bit as she dries, creams and helps Kathy to get dressed. She notices that Kathy's bottom is sore after all the diarrhoea and makes a note in the diary for workers to be extra careful about gentle cleaning and application of creams. (Workers are remarkably successful at keeping Kathy's skin in good condition with such a severe bowel problem. If it does break down it needs to be caught early, and often the best treatment is to lay her on her bed for periods with no pads, if possible in sunlight, and be even more vigilant about checking regularly for wetness and soiling.)

Kathy goes in the lounge with more music while Maureen sorts the washing out. Maureen pops in to check her and finds she has worked herself down on to the floor and over to collect some favourite objects. However when Maureen comes in five minutes later Kathy has fallen asleep. When she wakes later Maureen suggests a walk, and when Kathy sees her jacket she laughs and claps, obviously approving. The walk along the canal bank is pleasant with dappled sunlight through the trees and bushes, and interesting dogs and people to watch. Kathy stays alert but needs a rest when they get home. She is interested in lunch but does not manage to eat much.

During the afternoon she is very quiet, dozing at times and happy to sit with Lynette on the sofa listening to music. Lynette chats to Kathy reminding her that it is Friday and she will be taking her to her parents later for the weekend.

Kathy watches Lynette pack her wheelchair bag and complete the diary, and enjoys the taxi ride until she falls asleep. She wakes up at the door and gives her mum a big laugh and her happy 'dee' sound. Lynette comes in and explains to Kathy's parents what has been happening, and they note her poor appetite and the fit activity. They decide to see how she is this evening and take her to the GP if necessary tomorrow. Kathy meanwhile is exploring the living room and looking for favourite things. She shouts for attention and leans towards the cassette player; some Russian folk music meets with her approval. She is pleased to sit at the table and tries to eat but does not manage much, even with help. Her mum gives her a food supplement by tube with her medication. The evening is spent listening to music, looking at pop-up books and having cuddles. Kathy is ready for bed at 10.00 pm and manages a good look around her bedroom and some sounds of pleasure before nodding off as she has her medication and fluids.

Her parents have been in bed for a couple of hours when they hear Kathy crying over the intercom. Her mum finds her very uncomfortable after a large bowel movement. After being cleaned and changed Kathy settles back to sleep. There is a repeat performance about two hours later and it is dad's turn this time. At 6.00 am Kathy has a series of loose bowel movements and is very shaky. Her mum decides to give her some Dioralyte (sugar and salt solution) to keep her electrolyte balance and avoid dehydration after all this diarrhoea. Both her parents and Kendal House keep stocks of this to use as necessary. Kathy refuses breakfast and is not very happy. She has her medication split four ways with small amounts of fluid at a time, and after an hour and a half is more settled. She tolerates a bath although she becomes very shaky again and has flickering eye movements. She now has a runny nose, and her parents decide she should be checked by the GP.

They ring the surgery at 9.00 am and are told to come round half an hour later. Saturday surgery is only for urgent cases, but Kathy's GP is prepared to see her at any time her carers consider she needs checking. He takes her temperature, checks her eyes, ears and throat against severe protests, and listens carefully to her chest. He says he cannot hear anything on her chest, but he and her parents are aware that because Kathy has a poor air intake, she could have an infection, the signs of which were not obvious on the stethoscope. Her eyes, ears and throat seem fine, and her temperature is normal. However, because Kathy takes steroids and aspirin, her temperature is rarely high even when she is ill, as her natural inflammatory responses to infection are suppressed by the medication. Her parents point out her poor appetite for several days, and the fact that the diarrhoea is worse than usual.

Kathy has got over her crossness at being examined, and is now smiling and responding to the doctor, whom she has known for several years. After discussion it is decided not to give her antibiotics at this stage, partly because the diarrhoea is so bad and they could make it worse, but also because it is not absolutely clear that she has an infection. The GP suggests that if she does not improve within twenty-four hours she should go to casualty for an X-ray to check for a chest infection. It could just be that her bowel disease is active for some reason and this is causing the problems. It is really a process of elimination of various possibilities and careful monitoring of any problems as Kathy can become very ill very quickly.

Kathy goes home for a clean and change and some more Dioralyte. Her parents decide to take her shopping, which she usually enjoys. She does for the first half hour but then gets tired and irritable and is pleased to get home. She chooses some small dolls to play with and settles happily to listen to some music. She is happy to sit at the table for lunch but does not manage to eat. She has some food supplement by tube and later some more Dioralyte. During the afternoon she enjoys watching the dusting and hoovering, has a snooze and enjoys rolling table tennis balls across the floor.

Her parents tell her that friends are expected for a meal this evening, and Kathy is delighted when they arrive, edging over the floor to greet them, examine their shoes and get them to roll her table tennis balls back. She enjoys the sociable atmosphere at the table and manages a little food. By the time the friends leave she is very tired, but manages a smile goodbye. The diarrhoea is a little better and she has Dioralyte again with tonight's medication given in several stages. She settles to sleep and this time sleeps through the night.

SUNDAY
Kathy is stirring at 7.00 am and needs a big clean up. She has some flickering eye episodes but generally seems more settled. Breakfast gets a big smile and she manages to eat most of it herself. Her bowel movements seem a little less loose, but her mum gives her some Dioralyte as well as soya, and splits the feeds. After a rest Kathy is pleased to get into the bath. She has her usual

flickering eye movements and is a little floppy when she comes out, but she splashed a bit and enjoyed a game with her motor boat. Her mum talks to her while she dries and creams her, and does physio, explaining that they are going to visit Kathy's grandma today. Kathy chooses between two dresses and has some warm tights put on.

She watches with interest as her wheelchair bag is packed, medication checked, spare nappies loaded, and some presents for her grandma put in a box. She helps to put her warm jacket on and laughs as she is wheeled up the ramp into the van. She flops out soon after which often happens now with a change of position. Her mum has put on her neck collar which supports her head when she is floppy, but before they go on the motorway her parents decide to stop and lift her out so she can sit next to her mum and lean on her until she comes round. She goes into a proper sleep and wakes later to look around with interest at the journey. Her grandma lives about eighty miles away in the Midlands, and Kathy has worked out the familiar signs that help her understand it is this particular journey today. When the van reaches the outskirts of her grandma's town Kathy shows signs of excitement, and she gives a big welcome smile as she is wheeled up the path where her grandma is waiting by the door.

Kisses and cuddles all round are followed by anxious looks and some small grumbling sounds from Kathy, who expects a meal after a longish journey to someone's house. Grandma has this all organised and Kathy's food is on the table within five minutes. Kathy manages to eat about half of it herself, and is persuaded to eat a little more with help. She then sits on her mum's lap while everyone else eats, enjoying the company. Afterwards her grandma gives her a box of favourite objects she keeps for Kathy, and these are examined carefully and everyone is invited to join in some games with them.

During the afternoon Kathy has some more diarrhoea but less copious than yesterday, and some trembling and flickering eyes, but these do not develop into anything worse. She enjoys a walk out to the local country park, especially along the woodland paths where there is dappled sunshine.

Goodbyes are said to grandma and Kathy sleeps for much of the journey back to London. Her parents take her straight back to Kendal House where Lynette gets a snack ready to offer her. Kathy and Victoria give each other their usual sidelong glances of recognition, and later they enjoy some music together.

Kathy seems more settled, and at present the fear of a chest or other infection has receded. She has managed to find the energy to enjoy the activities of the weekend. However, her parents and support workers are aware of how vulnerable she is, and how carefully the details of her care must be managed. It is a matter of getting the balance right so that she is helped to do the activities she enjoys, but monitored carefully to try to pick up the signs of impending illness before she goes down with a serious infection.

A WEEK IN THE LIFE OF VICTORIA

MONDAY

The day starts off with Victoria giving Tracy one of her huge, dazzling smiles, as a welcome to the morning. Tracy is one of Victoria's team of workers and she has brought in her medication and a cup of tea at 8.15 am. (Her pills must be given at set times throughout the day to ensure maximum anti-convulsant effect.) Victoria is in bed, and although she has been awake for some time, has been lying quietly waiting. She takes the medication well, and gulps down her tea; Tracy begins to prepare Victoria for the day. She helps Victoria out of bed onto the shower chair, and wheels her into her shower room. Here she undresses her, and Victoria pulls off her nightdress with her right hand. Tracy showers her quickly, telling her what she is doing all the time. Victoria goes back to the bedroom to be dried and has various creams applied to her body to keep her skin in good order. Tracy then puts on her body brace and calipers, dresses her and brushes her long dark brown hair and puts it in a pony tail. Getting ready for the day can take up to two hours; it very much depends on Victoria's mood or condition.

Tracy then helps Victoria walk to the kitchen. In the house Victoria is encouraged to walk with assistance everywhere. She sits in the kitchen and watches Tracy very carefully as her breakfast is prepared. Tracy talks to her constantly, telling her the egg is ready, only waiting for the toast. Coffee is made. Victoria needs prompting when eating by herself and although she gets messy is pleased with her achievement.

After breakfast, and teeth cleaning, Victoria walks into the lounge to sit in her specially adapted armchair, which accommodates her scoliosis. As she cannot read or appreciate television, her main activities whilst alone are listening to music, flicking certain favourite pieces of paper and handling an assortment of objects that usually make a noise, such as an empty plastic lemonade bottle filled with beans. Tracy gives her some paper and asks her to wait whilst she strips the bed, puts the washing on and carries out a few other domestic chores.

Once these are done, she tells Victoria it is her turn to shop today for food for herself and Lisa. So she puts on her coat, helps her into the wheelchair and they go to Sainsbury's and the market. Victoria is glad to be out, and laughs out loud as the wind and rain touch her face. She looks with interest at the other shoppers and if one takes her fancy, reaches to touch an interesting bag or coat. As she buys her fruit and vegetables from a stall, the stall holder shares a joke with both women, and each one comes away with a handful of grapes and 'Have a nice day, Vicky'. On the way home, Victoria loves to touch things like railings, glass windows and cement bollards. They are greeted by 'Hi there' from Sean the caretaker as they come onto the estate.

Time for lunch, which on this occasion, is not appreciated by Victoria, so it is left covered on the side. She may be hungry later on. Victoria begins to moan. This is one way she communicates, another is by eye pointing. Usually the moans mean she wants something, is bored, or needs changing. Tracy decides to lay her down on the carpet in the lounge to rest, and listen to her Flying Pickets music. This is obviously what she wanted, and Tracy begins the hand-over to the next shift worker, Rose. After about an hour, Victoria decides she feels able to sit up, and looks expectantly at Rose, who asks if she would like some lunch now.

While Victoria is finishing off her toast, the chiropodist calls to see her and Lisa. Victoria very much enjoys the experience of someone pampering her delicate and somewhat misshapen feet. The chiropodist recommends foot massage and wearing socks at night to help with circulation and to prevent chilblains. Victoria often bites the right palm of her hand, and a callous has formed. The chiropodist recommends applying a skin softener, and gently using a pumice stone.

Sunshine breaks through, so Rose decides to take Victoria out for a short walk for some fresh air. They walk to Euston Station, and sit on the concourse – people watching. There is the usual throng of people, but today there is extra activity, police with dogs are striding about. The air is charged with excitement, and although it's not obvious why there is all this activity, Victoria loves it and watches everyone. The weather is changing, so off they go back home. Victoria doesn't mind, and continues to shout with glee.

Both women enjoy a cup of tea together, and then Victoria watches Rose sort out the washing, put it into the machine, iron what is ready, and put away clothes in her bedroom. She then watches Rose prepare the evening meal of shepherd's pie and vegetables, which she is sharing with Lisa tonight. They seem to enjoy this and look at each other briefly throughout the meal. Lisa supervises the washing up, but Victoria is restless and has to lie down quietly in her bedroom. After returning to the lounge she sits in her armchair flicking her favourite paper, and being encouraged to tap various objects with a plastic bat. Her workers have to find suitable things for her that are not too heavy or dangerous, that she can tap or handle constantly to give her pleasure. Recently a worker with insight replaced the shining paper in her wheelchair bag with a heavy duty small manila envelope. This looks much more appropriate and comforts and amuses Victoria while she is out.

At 9 pm Victoria has her medication with a cup of Horlicks and Rose begins the wind down for the day. This is the only part of the day when Victoria is without her body brace, and she enjoys the freedom and feel of her own skin. Time then for a relaxing bath in special oil to keep her skin in good condition. This is followed by a lovely massage tonight from Rose; Victoria really enjoys this. She is then helped into bed, and shows she is pleased to be there, giggling with delight. Her music tonight is Vivaldi – goodnight Victoria.

TUESDAY

Begins with a groan; unfortunately Victoria had a restless night having two seizures, and she makes it clear that she does not want to take her pills or get up. Rose decides, after seeing that Victoria is very disorientated and floppy, just to give her pills and tea, change her and leave her to sleep off the aftermath of the heavy seizures.

Around 10.30 am Victoria begins to stir, so it's time for the daily shower routine. Today Victoria is not co-operative and does not help by putting her arms in her clothes. She appears irritable and often tries to pull Rose's hair, or give her a swift pinch. She begins to pluck her own hair, so Rose tries diversion and walks her swiftly to the kitchen. Eventually the Weetabix and toast are eaten, but Victoria needs encouragement and patience today. Lisa and her worker have gone shopping and Victoria has to wait in for the council workmen. The intercom and shower need urgent repairs, and when eventually one man arrives Victoria looks with interest at his tool box and what he is doing.

At 12.30 it is staff handover time and Sharon begins her shift. After a snack lunch it is time for the first adult education class of the week which is Let's Make Music. The taxi arrives on time, and Victoria likes being in the vehicle. On arrival, she makes it clear that she would still like to be in the taxi and begins moaning. However, other people begin to arrive, and the jostling about diverts her. The class has seven students with learning disabilities. The young male teacher is a firm favourite of Victoria's and she flirts madly with her eyes. She really enjoys making music using many different instruments, and the hour goes very quickly.

Sharon thinks as it is a nice day she will walk Victoria home in her wheelchair. Victoria enjoys most of it, but doesn't like the stops today, and moans every time a traffic light is against her. On the way home she is greeted by three people who know her or the family.

Once home it is obvious that she needs changing and showering urgently; maybe that was what the moaning was for. Once she is fresh again she is brought into the kitchen for tea and company and to watch the evening meal being prepared, but Victoria does not want to, so it is back to the lounge to lie on the floor messing about with her 'box of tricks'. This large plastic container with her plastic bottles and plumber's plastic pipes gives her endless pleasure, either tapping or quietly handling the objects. Sometimes she throws them swiftly round the room when she is giving vent to something.

The evening meal does not go down well, and Sharon has to abandon the spaghetti. She offers biscuits and cheese, and fruit. The fruit is thrown, but the rest devoured quickly. As Victoria is very restless, Sharon helps her to put on her coat, get into the wheelchair and they go out for a walk round the block.

It is dark; Victoria likes being pushed along the Caledonian Road with its noisy traffic and perks up. The red buses, an ambulance, a fire engine and police cars provide plenty of activity to attract her full attention. She is glad to be back home and enjoys her bath, but soaks Sharon. She has her medication and Horlicks and as she seems tired, goes to bed early. The Everley Brothers' music sees her drifting off.

WEDNESDAY

Victoria is not too sure of today, and a half smile greets Sharon. It is also early, so Sharon explains it is a Stanmore day today and she has to get up early to leave the house a 9.30 am. To keep her scoliosis in check, Victoria wears her body brace for fourteen hours a day. She wears calipers and special boots to support her weak legs and ankles. Both often require adjusting and it is repairs to the brace that want attention today. Hence the need to visit the orthopaedic hospital at Stanmore.

After a very quick shower and breakfast, Victoria is ready at last, and sits patiently waiting looking out of her lounge window at her neighbours walking past. She sees Norman, her dad, arrive at the gate and gives him a smile, and is very pleased to see him as he comes into the house. After checking they have everything they need, for what might turn out to be a long hospital visit, they set off in Norman's car. Victoria is absolutely delighted to be out and about,and responds to her favourite Greek radio station on the car radio.

Victoria usually enjoys hospital visits as a family member always goes with the worker; she loves to watch people, and she is the centre of attention. Today she is in good form and responds well to the male technician who laughs and jokes with her. This visit only takes three hours and the return journey is smooth.

Lorna has come on duty and relieves Sharon. Victoria's lunch is already prepared, and she eats her meal with a minimum amount of support. After a lie down, she has to go out and buy milk and bread, and also a 21st birthday present for Lisa's birthday today. Upper Street is full of activity, noise and bustle, and Victoria takes great delight in helping select suitable cards and a video tape for Lisa.

She goes back home for Ann and Trudy, who are speech therapists and come to Victoria as volunteers. They are acting as Facilitator Communicators, and are carrying out a pilot study with Victoria using an unusual method of communication involving the use of letters of the alphabet on cards. Depending on her mood, Victoria usually enjoys the sessions, and today is no exception.

After Ann and Trudy have gone, Lorna gives Victoria a wash and change of clothes, brushes her hair and wheels her up to Lisa's family home twenty minutes walk away. Lisa and Victoria look at each other briefly, and then quickly look at everyone else in the room. Victoria's mum and sister are there and both give her a hug and a kiss. Although she does not return the affectionate welcome she does give lots of signs of recognition, and watches both women frequently. Lorna helps her sit on the settee and Victoria enjoys the supper buffet, two glasses of wine and one of champagne. She is very content sitting amongst her family and friends celebrating her flat mate's birthday. Her day is complete when dad arrives. Around nine, Lisa and Victoria are getting weary and Pauline (Lisa's mum) and the workers drive them back to their house. After a quick bath, medication and skin attention, it is time for bed.

THURSDAY

'Hi there everybody, I'm ready to get up.' If she had words this is what Victoria would be saying today by yelling at the top of her voice. She is very pleased to see Lorna, who is the same age as Victoria and they have a special rapport. Lorna explains during the shower/dressing routine that they have to go to the doctor to pick up her prescription as she has almost run out of pills. Victoria is in high spirits today and enjoys the walk to the surgery. The waiting rooms are small, and Victoria causes a stir as she topples a table over which was covered in leaflets which fly everywhere. A kindly soul offers to help and has her handbag snatched by Victoria. A little struggle takes place and Lorna has to restore order quickly. Some patients laugh, especially as the incident is taken lightly by the handbag lady, but some people are obviously uncomfortable and it shows on their faces. A child asks why she behaves so badly, and Lorna explains about the learning disability and Victoria's interests in life. The child is pleased with the explanation, gives Victoria a leaflet about Better Prostate Health, and helps Lorna by opening the doors – Lorna escapes with relief. A stall holder jokes about Victoria's leaflet as she shops in the market.

As it is not raining today, both women enjoy being out, and do a bit of window shopping. They have to return to the house for the lunchtime hand-over, and Rose is on duty again today. Victoria is impatient as the staff talk together, and moans, pulling her eyebrows together expressively. Eventually they finish and Rose gets her lunch. Pat from Flexi-Team arrives and Victoria is taken out for a walk down the canal tow path. After a short while it is clear that she does not want to be out and she starts moaning. After ten minutes the moans get louder and louder and she begins throwing her arms around and banging her feet on the foot rests of her wheelchair. Pat finds it increasingly difficult to control the wheelchair and returns as quickly as she can to the house. Victoria is now completely out of control and it takes her, Rose, and Lisa's worker to get her into bed, which is the safest place for her.

They take her boots and calipers off and arrange a bath towel round her arm to stop her biting herself. This episode is part of Victoria's seizure range, and it is thought that this particular seizure is hallucinatory which is very distressing and frightening for Victoria, and very demanding for her workers.

After about half an hour she gradually calms down, and because she is so exhausted she falls asleep. On waking an hour later, she has another partial complex seizure, which only lasts 20 seconds, and she comes round with a faint smile. She is brought into the lounge and Rose gives her a large cup of tea.

Rose then takes her into the kitchen, where Eva has prepared the evening meal of vegetable curry and chapattis. Victoria eats with relish and shouts for more. Rose gives her another helping.

Rose then takes her into the lounge, and it is obvious that Victoria does not want to do the floor activities with her, so Rose leaves her alone, but puts on her opera music.

Bath and bed are welcome, and tonight's music is Jazz Ladies with sandalwood oils giving a delightful smell throughout the house – goodnight.

A crash disturbs the house around midnight. Victoria has been learning to lift the side bar of her bed. This is six feet long, quite heavy, and fits into two grooves at the top and bottom of the bed. (This is to prevent Victoria falling out of bed.) Tonight not only has she lifted it out, but has managed to push it away from the bed, and it has caught a chest of drawers. Rose makes sure Victoria is all right, puts the bar back and ties it with tapes, as a temporary measure. She clears the debris from the floor, and Victoria gives her one of her huge dazzling overwhelmingly beautiful smiles, turns over and snuggles under the duvet. Rose returns to her bed. Goodnight again, Victoria.

FRIDAY

Calmly waiting for the handmaiden, Victoria surveys the damage to her bedroom, and greets Rose with a warm smile. Another quick shower/breakfast routine as it is adult education class, and today it is wheelchair dancing. There is a bit of a flap as the taxis booked last night do not turn up on time and Rose and Lisa's workers have to phone around rapidly to find alternatives. Victoria travels by mini cab, but it looks as if Lisa will be unable to go as her wheelchair does not fold down to go in a boot.

Victoria loves the wheelchair session, particularly as loud music with a strong beat is played and she enjoys meeting other people she knows. Annie, the teacher, is a gem and shows great enthusiasm and style, which encourages the young people to really enjoy the sessions. Victoria is assisted to dance with two people guiding her arms and she is in her element, bopping to Dire Straits.

Home, and lunch is refused again. Victoria has a lie down on the lounge carpet, with music. Trina is on duty today and more food and toilet roll shopping is required. Once Victoria looks ready for a move, Trina puts her coat on, and off they go. They both window shop, and Victoria goes in to buy a shirt. The assistant is somewhat hesitant at first, but the huge smile wins her over and she becomes most helpful. Victoria chooses a red and green shirt.

Back home for tea, and just as Victoria finishes, her mum arrives. Victoria is so pleased to see her, and greets her with yells. Jean has come to pay Victoria's weekly money into the house and personal kitties and update the simple account books. She also wants to talk about Victoria's week and just to be with her. After the money business Jean reads Victoria's diary and catches up on what has been happening. She talks to both Victoria and Trina about her week, and makes a note that the bed panel requires attention. She will tell Norman, who will have to devise some method to stop Victoria removing the panel. Trina tells Jean that something is wrong with Victoria who seems unwell; she is sometimes refusing food, but Trina can't really identify what is wrong. Victoria has no words, and cannot indicate an area, even if she is in the greatest pain. Jean re-reads the diary for the previous two weeks and questions workers closely about Victoria's pattern of behaviour. Eventually she suggests that a urine sample be taken first thing in the morning, and then taken immediately to the doctor. She also writes up in Victoria's diary that all workers should monitor how Victoria looks, if she has a temperature, what food she is eating, and offer her more drinks all the time. Regarding her health, experience has taught everyone connected with Victoria that nothing must be left to chance, things must always be rigorously checked, as Victoria can become very ill very quickly.

Jean spends a few hours in the house, the last part just lying, cradling Victoria's head and shoulders in her lap. Victoria loves these times and is quiet and content just laying, looking and listening to her mum. Jean leaves as the bath routine begins. Victoria is relaxed and happy and Jean is content to have seen her daughter – goodnight Victoria.

SATURDAY

Victoria meets the day with a wan smile, and does not want her tea. After some difficulty, Trina manages to get her medication down, although it is apparent she is not well. Also after a lot of difficulty she eventually manages to get a urine sample and decides to take this and Victoria to the doctor that morning. So a quick shower, dress and breakfast and up to the doctor, which operates an emergency system on Saturdays. The friendly receptionist is on today, and there is only a short wait with Victora getting more and more grumpy and lethargic. The doctor sees her and decides it might be a urinary infection; he puts her on antibiotics, and will get her sample tested. On the way back home they collect the antibiotics from the chemists.

Once home Victoria makes it clear she really does not want to do anything or be with anyone, and just lies on the floor. Trina covers her with a blanket, and gets on with household chores, popping back to see her often. Victoria sleeps for a few hours, which is most unusual in the daytime. Sharon comes on duty, and Trina gives her the full picture of what has been happening to Victoria. She refuses her lunch again, but drinks some cranberry and raspberry juice recommended by her sister Tara as good for urinary infections. Sharon puts her in her armchair, but she has no energy. She offers her different things to touch and handle, but Victoria is not very interested. After a little while her head droops and she begins to cry and Sharon decides to give her a paracetamol tablet and put her to bed for a while. Victoria is grateful for being in her bed and just lies quietly listening to her music. Sharon telephones Victoria's mum to tell her what is happening and says she does not think Victoria is well enough to go swimming this afternoon with her. For the rest of the day and evening Victoria stays in her bed and bedroom, while Sharon takes the opportunity of sorting her clothes and personal items in her bedroom. The house seems very quiet without Victoria's sounds. She gives Victoria a shower instead of a bath, but asks Lisa's worker to help her as Victoria is so floppy and not co-operative. Victoria is glad to be back in bed again and goes to sleep listening to Bing Crosby.

SUNDAY

Victoria is awake when Sharon comes in, but no smiles today. She is very thirsty, and drinks two cups of tea straight down, a good sign. Sharon gives her a bath to make up for last night, but Victoria only half heartedly gives a few splashes, just to keep up her reputation as a splasher. Sharon attempts to offer some scrambled egg, but only a small piece of toast is acceptable today. Later in the morning Sharon wheels Victoria to the local shop to get some milk and for a walk round the block, but Victoria wilts over the side of her wheelchair.

Once home Sharon lies Victoria on the sofa. She lies flicking paper or just looking round the room. Jean and Norman arrive at 3 pm as they have all been invited to tea at Maria and Mike's house. (Maria has been a friend of Victoria's for four years, since she was a volunteer on the Kith and Kids projects.) Maria has recently had a baby and wants to show him off to Victoria. Jean decides that maybe a little visit out will cheer Victoria up, and if not she will bring her straight home. In the car, Victoria does begin to look out of the window and shows some interest as they walk her up to Maria's house. She sits content on the sofa, but shows no interest in Philip, the new baby. Mum holds her hand, and as Maria has brought all Victoria's favourite foods, crisps, cheese biscuits and pretzels, she offers them to Victoria, who takes them and begins to eat. Maria also offers Victoria some paper she has been saving for her, and this meets with approval. Only when Philip makes his own baby noises or cries does Victoria show any interest. But she recognizes Maria and is pleased to be in company with lively conversation.

The Sunday afternoon tea invitation has certainly cheered her up, but she is glad to be back home. Sunday evening Sharon and Judith decide to lay the table in the lounge as Lisa and Victoria will eat together tonight. Although Victoria does not eat much, probably having had too many crisps in the afternoon, she likes the atmosphere, and looks a little better.

After the usual bath/skin routine it is time for bed, and Victoria is glad to be there; she looks so relieved that she is feeling better. Sharon sorts out her favourite Mozart music, and Victoria smiles 'thanks and goodnight'.

The actual names of support workers have not been used in the above accounts.

CHAPTER 8

BEREAVEMENT AND REPLACEMENT

There was a brief reference in the Operational Policy to the eventuality of one of the tenants moving out. No criteria were given for replacement and there were no details of procedures. There was a similarly brief reference in the Service Agreement.

No one imagined that this situation would arise only four months after the project started, and in such sad circumstances.

Kathy had been less well than usual during 1991. She was admitted to hospital in August but was not felt by her doctors to be seriously ill. Suddenly she developed pneumonia, and died within days. Her parents had been with her constantly, and Jean and Norman were visiting her at the time of her death.

The shock and overwhelming grief at Kathy's death can only be imagined by those who have suffered a comparable loss. It was made worse because the doctors caring for her were either not aware of how ill she was, or chose not to convey their knowledge to her parents, so there was no expectation or preparation for her death. Her parents felt her last hours were managed in a muddled and inconsistent way, and worried that the process of dying for Kathy may have been unnecessarily frightening and painful.

Apart from these particular circumstances, the relationship between Kathy and her parents was necessarily very close, and her death was bound to be devastating for them.

Kathy's relationship with many other friends, and especially with Jean and Norman, was also very strong, and friends and support workers alike were deeply affected by her death. A group of friends helped Pat and Barrie to organise the funeral as a celebration of Kathy's achievements. Over two hundred and fifty friends and carers wrote to express their grief and many of those attended her funeral.

Victoria attended Kathy's funeral, and was unusually quiet during the proceedings, crying out only when everyone sat silently reflecting on what Kathy's life had meant for them. Victoria's family, friends and support workers talked to her about Kathy's illness and death, but could not be sure how much she understood.

However much or little Victoria understood, it was to become very clear to her that Kathy was no longer there as weeks and then months went by when she was alone in the house, apart from her support worker. Eventually she must have realised that Kathy was not coming back. This was an unhappy and isolating situation for both Victoria and her workers.

For the first few weeks after Kathy died it was difficult for Pat and Barrie to think of anything but their grief. Even getting through the routine tasks of each day was a struggle. Jean and Norman were reluctant to raise the issue of Victoria's isolation. They did not want to hurt Pat and Barrie, but they also found it painful even to contemplate replacing Kathy with another tenant. Other close friends were aware of the situation, and urged Jean and Norman to find the right time to raise the subject. Jean and Norman felt they had to talk to Pat and Barrie before contemplating any move.

The parents' network in Islington was a very close one. These parents had shared their problems with their children's disabilities, fought together to improve services, supported one another through crises and received support when they needed it.

A couple who knew Kathy's and Victoria's families very well, Pauline and Tony Davis, had a daughter, Lisa. She was now eighteen, and had profound intellectual and multiple disabilities. Pauline's back was damaged through lifting over the years, and she was also pregnant. Lisa spent regular periods in respite care, and Pauline and Tony felt sure she was ready for a more independent life style.

Hesitantly, the three couples met one evening at Jean and Norman's home. Jean and Norman were obviously concerned at the isolation of Victoria and her support workers, and were also worried that the project would not be viable unless another tenant could be found. They also found the burden of managing affairs at the house very heavy after their close co-operation with Pat and Barrie.

Pauline and Tony had many questions to ask – about the care package, the finances and the way the house was managed. Both couples were very sensitive to the feelings of Pat and Barrie, who in turn felt it was vital, however difficult it was to find the words, to give their support to enabling the project to survive.

Pauline and Tony lost no time in contacting their social worker and applying to the ILF. Social Services obviously had to be involved in the arrangements for a replacement tenant. They had no mechanism for doing this, and simply looked at lists, at one point suggesting that a young man should move in. Jean and Norman had to assert Victoria's right to a compatible replacement. In the particular context of Victoria's disabilities and the arrangements in the house, they did not feel it was appropriate for her co-tenant to be male. Victoria was a tenant of the council in her own right, and therefore could expect to exercise choice as to who the other tenant should be. It was reasonable to interpret this through the involvement of her parents.

This was a very difficult and delicate period in terms of negotiations. It was quite right that Social Services should be overseeing procedures for replacement as they would be part-funding the care costs. However, they did not seem to have any coherent plan for doing this nor to have any sensible suggestions. Pauline and Tony made it clear that they would be asking for full time residential provision for Lisa very soon anyway, and pointed out that if Lisa went to live at Kendal House it would cost the local authority less. Moreover, Lisa and Victoria always got on well together. Lisa and Victoria had comparable levels of disability, so the physical environment of the house would be appropriate for Lisa. Further, the two young women had known each other practically all their lives. They each had their own distinct interests, but also shared some preferences such as good food, discos, parties and outings.

No other suitable candidate emerged. Indeed, if one had, it would have been hard work for anyone to match Pauline and Tony's persistence in obtaining the ILF funding and going through the various formalities. Even so, it was over six months before Lisa moved in to Kendal House.

THE EFFECTS ON VICTORIA

Kathy's death

Kathy and Victoria had known each other for fifteen years. They had visited one another's homes frequently, got to know one another's wider families, been on holiday together with their families, been involved together in their parents' campaigns to improve services, notably the setting up of Field End House, one of the first residential units to care for children with profound intellectual and multiple disabilities in a home-like setting in their own community. They lived together at Field End House for five years, and through their families kept in close touch when Kathy had to leave at the age of nineteen for an adult residential unit. They shared difficulties, visiting each other in hospital, and happy times, celebrating birthdays, Christmas and other special occasions together.

They shared many interests, but each maintained a sturdy independence, often watching the other out of the corner of one eye while planning some wickedness.

No one really knows what went through Victoria's mind when Kathy first went away, and then as weeks and months passed, did not come back. Jean and Norman thought it was important for her to attend Kathy's funeral so she had the opportunity to experience the formal farewell to her friend, and the mixing with family and close friends immediately afterwards. But Victoria had no means of conveying her own feelings, or even asking the questions she must have had.

Over the next months Victoria was often more distressed than usual, and it was difficult to know how much this was grief, and how much the increased isolation, changes in her support workers and indeed the results of her complex epilepsy. All her parents and support workers could do was to continue to talk to her about Kathy. Kathy's photo stayed in the living room, and a music centre was installed with money from donations given instead of flowers. This was marked by a gathering for the families, friends and former carers on what would have been Kathy's 28th birthday, held at the house.

With all this, there is no doubt that Victoria has had to cope with her thoughts and feelings without the opportunity of sharing them, the most elementary stage in dealing with grief.

The isolation

As soon as Kathy died, her funding for care was stopped and her support workers were redeployed. Victoria continued to have one support worker during waking hours, and someone to sleep in. This was a difficult situation for both her and the workers. There was much to do – personal care for Victoria, shopping and cooking, washing and cleaning the house – as well as finding meaningful activities for Victoria. There was no one else in the house to chat with, or ask for advice or help, or share a joke.

Kathy and Victoria had by no means done everything together, but shared outings and activities were part of a varied range of experiences, and it was often easier to organise these if two support workers were involved. It was now more likely that Victoria and her support workers would suffer bore-dom. Much of the knowledge and training in the caring role of the support workers comes from sharing experiences, and the lack of opportunity for this limited their development during this period. Inevitably, they had to fall back on asking Jean and Norman for advice more frequently.

OTHER ISSUES

The grief of the support workers

Some of Kathy's support workers had known her for some years. Even those who had only worked with her recently had formed strong bonds with her. Caring for her was very hard work – physically, as her personal care was so demanding with constant diarrhoea and tube feeding – and emotionally draining as she was often in pain and discomfort and suffered dangerous epileptic attacks. But through such close physical contact, communication developed, and Kathy was very appreciative when she felt carers got it right. She could be very obstinate and assertive at times, but her sense of humour, deep laugh and lovely smile made up for the difficult times.

All Kathy's support workers were deeply moved by her death, and some found it hard to cope with their grief. They wrote movingly to Pat and Barrie about what Kathy had meant to them. After such a close and meaningful relationship it must have been very difficult for those who had to move quickly on to work with someone else. Those who continued to work with Victoria had daily reminders of Kathy's life in the house.

Some asked for a particular doll or toy to remember Kathy by, or photographs, and continued to keep in touch with Pat and Barrie.

Although in this job workers can expect death to occur frequently among the people they care for, this does not necessarily make it any easier for them to cope with the experience.

Perhaps there should be preparatory work to help develop an awareness of what it might mean personally when the death occurs of someone you have been working with so closely. Certainly there should be structured support immediately afterwards, and the offer of further help if a particular worker feels it is needed.

Pat and Barrie received much sympathy and support from Kathy's carers and were able in turn to offer continued contact and discussion. The mutual nature of this process reflected the warmth and closeness that had developed when all were working together with Kathy.

Of course workers have to go on doing their job with someone else, but it seems right for them to feel that it is appropriate to express their feelings, when given the opportunity, and for this to be seen as a natural stage in coming to terms with a very real loss to them. They may feel angry or bewildered about particular events before death, and their thoughts must be allowed expression if they are to have any chance of settling things in their minds.

The grief felt by Jean and Norman

Jean and Norman offered unconditional support to Pat and Barrie at the time of Kathy's death. But they themselves were overwhelmed with the events of the last days before she died, and with the realisation of her death. People who saw it as the death of 'your friend's daughter' did not understand the particular closeness of the relationship; it was as near to losing their own child as was possible. Kathy's death also reminded them of how vulnerable Victoria and those like her are. Some close friends realised the hugeness of the loss for Jean and Norman, and were able to offer recognition and support for this. But they had to cope with this grief as they still had to get on with the day-to-day cares of running the house, and Victoria, and the concerns of the rest of their family.

The burden of running the house for one family

The idea and planning of the house, and the practical realities of getting it running and keeping it going, had been shared by both families. Now Pat and Barrie found it hard even to visit the house to see Victoria, and Jean and Norman found themselves bearing the whole burden.

This brought home the realisation that the management structures were inadequate to support the smooth running of the house. Jean and Norman had to cope with managing Victoria's household budget and personal expenses, monitoring her personal care including her physiotherapy, checking that attention was paid to her developmental needs such as toilet training, developing a more effective system of communication, seeing that her epilepsy was monitored and that seizures were dealt with appropriately, trouble shooting when appliances or the heating system broke down, chasing the neighbourhood office for repairs, ensuring bills were paid, liaising with the GP, OT and physiotherapist, co-ordinating arrangements for hospital appointments and supporting the support workers who felt isolated and often anxious. Working with Pat and Barrie, they had been able to share the work out, and have a joke when things became difficult.

Now at times all this responsibility seemed an intolerable burden, and the excitement and hope about the project was hard to rekindle.

Anticipating this situation in similar projects

Parents who care for people with profound intellectual and multiple disabilities live with the daily reality of health crises, and may have seen the person they care for through several life-threatening episodes. Those whose profession is to care for people with this degree of disability know they are more prone to some illnesses and that aspects of their condition can deteriorate.

The experience of the parents in this case shows that it is better to anticipate the possibility of the death of one of the tenants in such an independent living project, and to make provision for managing it in the Operational Policy and management systems. This may sound morbid to some – but it is only voicing the possibility that is in the minds of all those who know the disabled person. The parents also felt that while nothing can mitigate the grief of those who are bereaved, neither is it any help to those who are grieving if the practical consequences of the death cause confusion and affect the lives of remaining tenants adversely.

If Kathy's struggles for independence were to mean anything now her own life was over, her achievement in becoming a tenant in her own home must not be lost. So what would help in similar situations?

1. There should be full details of procedures to be followed in the event of the departure of one of the tenants, including their death. These should include agreed ground rules about the procedure and criteria for replacement, with clear management mechanisms. If these details are agreed beforehand, then those who are grieving will not be pressured into agreeing to decisions which may be inappropriate, and those remaining in the house will be less likely to suffer a long period of reduced staffing and isolation. A possible framework for such ground rules is given at the end of this chapter; they would need to be incorporated in the Operational Policy, and accepted as an elaboration of the very basic statement on this issue made in the Service Agreement.

2. Parents, support workers, family and friends should be encouraged to voice any feelings or fears they have about the person they care for. With support workers this will need to be structured as part of on-going training. Family, friends and representatives of the disabled person need to be involved so they can talk about any earlier crises and share their feelings. This will not be easy and cannot be forced. Not all family, friends and representatives will have been able to put their innermost fears into words, and some may prefer not to. The importance of a good and trusted social worker could be crucial here,

in drawing out these issues. When family and friends are reticent, this must be respected, but support workers should still be offered the chance to discuss these matters.

3. If one of the tenants becomes seriously ill, full information should be given to all support workers, and subject to the wishes of the family of the person who is ill, the other tenants and their families should be made aware. Support workers should talk to the other tenants about the situation and if possible and appropriate, should take them to visit in hospital.

4. If a death occurs, everyone involved should be given clear and basic information as soon as possible. Support workers need to talk to the other tenants about what has happened, and should not be afraid to show their own feelings. It may be helpful to show photographs of the person who has died when explaining that they will not be coming back to the house.

5. The funeral arrangements will be of great significance in helping the family and support workers to accept the death. Some families will have strong religious beliefs which will govern the form the funeral arrangements and service will take. It is of the greatest importance for the other tenants and support workers to attend the funeral, and this will need to be handled sensitively with the families of the other tenants, and must of course be in agreement with the family of the person who has died. Involving the other tenants in writing cards of condolence, arranging flowers if there are to be any, and any other arrangements, will all be helpful in conveying what has happened. If the bereaved family can invite the other tenants and support workers to any social gathering after the funeral, this will also help them to feel the reality of what has happened.

    Opportunities should be taken afterwards to talk about the person who has died, to remember good times together, and to express sadness. None of this will be easy. But it is better to try, even if mistakes are made, than to leave those who cannot communicate their feelings verbally with no opportunity to try and understand what has happened. Those managing the house have a crucial role to play here, and should be well prepared before a death occurs.

6. When a replacement tenant arrives, there must be great sensitivity to how they take over the room of the one who has died. Pat and Barrie went to the house some weeks after Kathy had died. They sorted out

mementos according to the expressed wishes of the support workers. They took home Kathy's personal things and the clothes which had the most memories. They arranged for the other clothes to go to people who had some connection with Kathy or with her workers. They left Kathy's special bed and other items in case her eventual replacement could make use of them. Victoria's family talked to her about Lisa coming to the house once it was certain, but in retrospect much more preparation could have been done for this by all concerned with Victoria. Now, all those most affected by Kathy's death recognise that they were so overwhelmed by their own feelings that they did not give sufficient consideration to how Victoria might have been affected.

POSSIBLE GROUND RULES IN THE EVENT OF A TENANT MOVING AWAY OR DYING

1. The representatives of each tenant who moves in to the house will agree on her/his behalf to the procedures outlined below, as part of the Operational Policy. These procedures are those referred to in the Service Agreement, and will be put into force when necessary by those responsible for managing the house.

2. When a tenant moves away from the house for any reason, or dies, this information will be shared with other tenants and their representatives as soon as the managers are aware of it.

3. The criteria for a replacement tenant are as follows:

    (Details to be inserted according to the particular circumstances of the house, eg. female only may be acceptable, the nature of the facilities may require tenants with a particular level of disability, etc.)

4. The procedures for identifying potential new tenants and selecting those who will take up the tenancy will be as follows:

    (To be agreed in accordance with the management structures in force for the house, ie. is it a local authority tenancy, a charitable foundation, etc.)

5. Before a tenant is finally accepted, (s)he will visit the house to meet the other tenants. The representatives of the other tenants will convey their interpretations of the wishes of those they represent to the body making the final decision. If there is disagreement, there will be an agreed system of mediation.

6. If a tenant moves to another residential setting, those tenants who wish to keep in touch with her/him will be enabled to do so by their support workers and representatives.

7. If a tenant has died, as far as is compatible with the wishes of their family and representatives, other tenants should be involved in funeral and memorial arrangements. Support workers should discuss the death and its implications with those they care for, and should encourage families and friends to do the same. They should seek professional advice such as bereavement counselling for other tenants if they feel this is necessary; this should be done with the agreement of the family and representatives of the tenants. Tenants and their representatives may feel it is important to record the memory of the person who has died, perhaps by keeping their photograph displayed, or retaining some of their possessions in the house, if the family agrees.

8. The family and representatives of the tenant who has died must not be rushed in the process of clearing out effects, and must be offered help in doing this if they wish.

CHAPTER 9

DIFFICULTIES AND SUCCESSES

This chapter discusses some of the problems which arose once the project became reality, and highlights some of the successful aspects.

THE CARE PACKAGE

Because this was a new approach to the care and support of people with very profound learning disabilities there were no models to build on. The closest comparison, and the one that was essentially used by the management of the care agency, was with the approach used for people with physical disabilities in similar projects. This was useful in some respects and detrimental in others. For example, it was good to build the project on notions of respect for the individual, the need for privacy and the right to enjoy an active and interesting lifestyle. However, the notion that someone with the degree of intellectual disability and difficulty with communication of Kathy, Victoria or Lisa could direct staff in line with their wishes, and could take decisions about what to do and where to go, was completely unrealistic.

A balance has to be struck between the desirability of giving the women choice about their activities, the clothes they wear and the food they eat, and the recognition of their limited ability to make choices. Sometimes the interpretation made by staff about the choice made may have more to do with the staff's wishes than that of the women. Too much adherence to principles without fully understanding their implications can lead to actions which deprive rather than benefit the woman concerned. An example of this is where activity objects, such as bottles filled with beans attached to Victoria's wheelchair were removed on the grounds that they were not appropriate for someone of her age. Staff did not consider how they would feel if someone deprived them of a favourite activity, such as watching 'Neighbours', or playing the oboe. For a long time, no attempt was made to find a more suitable object, which would have given her as much pleasure.

This was eventually done by one perceptive worker who filled a little leather bag with coins and fixed it to her wheelchair. Victoria welcomed the new activity, and the workers felt the new arrangement was more appropriate. But in the meantime, her preferred choice had been denied.

On the issue of personal care, it was certainly true that Kathy, Victoria and Lisa let their workers know if they were unhappy. However, even those who had known them for a long time had to look and listen carefully, and often go through a process of elimination to find out whether it was a pad that needed changing, hunger or thirst, boredom or a desire for a change in environment and activity. In these circumstances support workers needed to be familiar with and to use the systems and procedures set up by the parents, referred to in Chapter 5 and discussed in more detail later in this chapter.

The complex personal and medical needs of these young women meant that meticulous attention to the details of agreed care procedures was essential if they were to remain well, safe and comfortable. Failure to pay careful attention to such procedures in one instance meant that one woman suffered considerable pain and discomfort. She developed skin irritation, apparently after unsuitable bath additives, soap and shampoo were used. She was prone to eczema and this developed rapidly until her legs were red, raw and weeping. This was not picked up at the earlier stage of irritation, when advice should have been sought. The incident illustrated how even a short period of carelessness could cause a rapid spiral downwards in the condition of someone with multiple disabilities.

MANAGEMENT ACCOUNTABILITY

The Principal Officer for Learning Difficulties wrote in 1990 that, 'the pace of activities had really grown faster than the…Department's procedures, and they (sic) recognised this'.

Because of the relative speed with which the project had been set up, no Operational Policy was agreed before the staff were appointed. This has been the cause of many problems since. Because the Social Services Department has no appropriate procedures in place, the draft Service Agreement has still not been agreed with the care agency. This has resulted in a lack of clarity about the roles of each person or agency involved, and about the decision-making process. It has also meant that there have been no reliable monitoring, recording or reviewing systems and that issues such as advocacy and the role of parents have not been effectively addressed. This lack of a formal structure has given rise to a feeling that the care agency is not accountable to either the local authority, the tenants or their parents. The vulnerability of the three women has reinforced this view, and has left the parents feeling that they are unequal partners in the process. This might have been overcome if the three women had all had allocated social workers throughout the period, but this has not been the case.

These difficulties were further compounded by the care agency's decision not to appoint a senior worker for the staff team, nor to identify key workers. With the three women's inability to communicate their views directly, and the complexity of their care packages, there has been a real need for one person to co-ordinate and act as a focal point for the staff team. The care agency has recently decided that there should be such a post.

COMMUNICATION

There has been disagreement, between staff and parents, about the interpretation of the needs and wishes of the women. Parents and friends have long experience of interpreting eye movements, body language, gestures and sounds. Communication is hard work on both sides, and the longer you know someone the more it improves. Parents have suggested ways in which staff can develop their skills of communication and interpretation, but they are naturally wary of staff who make their own interpretations from the basis of a short acquaintance. Examples of this have occurred in relation to non-emergency episodes of distress, which may be due to a headache, period pains or other discomfort, but have been interpreted as behaviour problems by some staff.

Communication amongst staff, and between them and others involved or working with the women, must be effective if complex needs are to be dealt with. Difficulties have arisen from the failure of some staff to use the information systems referred to earlier.

These consist of essential handbooks prepared by the parents, to be kept in the house. These provide information for staff on procedures and offer a framework for recording events. They are very thorough and clear. They are:

The Operational Policy	This underpins the whole care package and provides the frame-work and ground rules.
The Care Books	These provide details of all personal care and other needs for the women.
House Books	These contain detailed instructions for all household equipment and for the day to day management of the house.

The Vehicle Log Book	This gives instructions for the use and mainte-nance of the vehicle, and provides a record of use and service.
Personal Diary	This is for staff to record personal care such as nail cutting, toileting, giving medication; shopping required; and the general events and activities of the day, including any medical or other problems.
House Diary	This lists daily appointments, invitations, instructions such as collecting prescriptions, any deliveries, accidents, incidents or any-thing else affecting the house and its resi-dents.

Examples of some of these documents are given in the Appendices. While the parents would not claim that they are perfect, they do represent the accumulated experience and expertise of many years. Support workers, other professionals involved with Kathy, Lisa and Victoria, medical staff and volunteers all say how invaluable these books are. However, staff at all levels vary in their ability to use this resource effectively. Unless these systems are used consistently by all involved in giving support, reading the information carefully and noting events for the period they are working, breakdowns in communication and arrangements will occur.

The various information books and diaries cover most eventualities. However, they can never cover them all, and it has to be assumed that support workers will exercise common sense and initiative when dealing with unforeseen circumstances. Unfortunately, this has not always occurred, and time, energy and sometimes money have been wasted when, for example, staff have failed to report minor faults in the vehicle which have subsequently become major ones, or called out an engineer when the heating was not working, only to discover it was not switched on.

HOME-MAKING

Much importance is given in the project to the house being the women's home. Staff appointed are expected to have home-making skills. However, everyone has different styles and preferences for their own homes. Most of the staff are of a different generation from that of the parents, and their lack of appropriate home-making skills in some cases, and the varied range of life-styles displayed in a group of staff, have led to disagreements. The parents have become disheartened at some workers' failure to take responsibility for maintenance of equipment and the lack of security awareness in some cases, demonstrated by such actions as leaving windows open when everyone goes out.

STAFF

It has not always been easy to recruit staff of the desired calibre, or to keep them for long periods. It is unusual for someone to stay for more than two years: it is a very demanding job and it is possible for the best workers to burn out. One of the greatest difficulties experienced by the project has been this lack of continuity of staff. This has been aggravated by the continued use of relief staff, who may individually be of high calibre, but who are unfamiliar with the procedures of the house and with the needs of the women.

The staff team has also suffered from a lack of suitable training, management supervision and support. The budget for the scheme has no identified amount for training. What training has been given has, generally, been provided from within the care agency. If a budget were available, greater use could be made of outside trainers, who could inject fresh ideas and reinforce standards. There has also been a lack of interest in using the parents to provide training from their perspective and experience. At one stage, parents offered to provide training time by keeping their daughters at home until enough shifts had been covered to enable workers to be paid for attending a training session.

Induction for new staff has involved sharing a shift with a more experienced worker, and sometimes even this has not been possible. New and relief staff frequently say they have not been informed about vital elements of managing the house, and have not been shown the house books or personal diaries.

Much potential conflict arises from the fact that the women's home is also the staff's workplace. There have been occasions when workers behaved as they would in an office, making phone calls, which go on the tenants' bill, or smoking.

The communal use of the vehicle has resulted in a need for a higher than expected level of maintenance and repairs. This has put an extra and unplanned burden on the project's budget. Staff tend to treat the vehicle with less care than they would one they owned themselves.

There has also been a tendency to show a lack of accountability for money, as though it comes from a bottomless purse. Shopping is sometimes carried out in an extravagant way, buying expensive items or small amounts when bulk purchase would save money.

THE DESIGN OF THE SCHEME

Because the scheme is unique, there is no peer group in a similar project with whom the staff can share experiences. Working on a one-to-one basis can be very lonely for staff, and can reduce their confidence. Workers may spend periods of time on their own with either Victoria or Lisa, and may therefore have little opportunity to share problems or causes for celebration. There is also minimal time for mutual support.

INSTITUTIONAL ATTITUDES

Mention has been made of the tendency for some workers to treat the house as they would an office. This attitude may also develop into one of treating the house as an institution, which provides care for its residents. Because neither of the tenants can communicate verbally, it is very difficult for them to create an ambience in which the house is seen at all times as their private space. Some workers have asked for a television to be provided. This would be primarily for their use, since Victoria has no interest in television and Lisa is inclined to watch indiscriminately. The parents have resisted this request, because of their bad experiences in the past of hospitals and residential homes where the television was permanently on, ignored by residents but treated by the staff as a source of entertainment and interest.

FAMILY CONTACTS

While the families have celebrated having their daughters living so near them, this has not always been encouraged by the managers or workers on the project. Some workers have failed to recognise the life-styles of these families, who are closely involved with each other in the extended family network and constantly dropping in to each other's houses. There have been requests for prior notice to be given by telephone of intending visits. While parents recognise the sense of checking on the planned activities of their daughters before visiting, they also appreciate being able to drop in on the chance that their daughter will be in – and if she isn't, then they are pleased that she is out and about.

QUALITY OF LIFE

There can be absolutely no doubt that the quality of life for the three women who have been part of the project has improved overall. They have been treated more as individuals and given a higher status than they ever had in the various institutions in which they previously lived.

Their daily lives contain a wider range of experiences and a greater choice of activities. They are directly involved in the running of their own home and they draw considerable satisfaction from this. They receive far more individual attention from the staff and their personal possessions are better looked after.

The fact that they are living in their own home and not in a 'home' is of great importance.

PERSONAL DEVELOPMENT

Since moving into the house, there has been a marked increase in and development of their skills. For example, Victoria can now walk for short distances; Lisa is more willing to consider a greater variety of leisure pursuits, and a wider range of music. The communication skills of both women have improved – perhaps the most exciting development of all.

They have a wider awareness of things outside the home as a result of improved communication with their workers. They go to more places, and they are familiar with the local roads, shops and parks.

SOCIAL INVOLVEMENT

They have become highly visible within the local community, and are always greeted by many passers-by when they go out in their wheelchairs.

Because the house is so close to their parents' houses it is much easier for families and friends to be involved. This ensures that the parents are always aware of their daughters' state of wellbeing, and also enables the families to spend time together and to celebrate occasions such as birthdays.

COLLABORATION

The way in which the scheme was planned and developed is an excellent example of successful joint working between statutory agencies, independent sector agencies and parents. The project group was a model of good practice for planning when it was first set up. Reference has already been made to the commitment and hard work demonstrated by those involved in the group, which enabled the project to open within an unusually short time scale. Although it did not always work smoothly, it did provide a forum where issues could be shared and discussed. In retrospect, the project group should have continued to meet once the project was underway, as it was only after a period of operation that some of the key issues, especially those of management and accountability, began to emerge.

CHAPTER 10

LESSONS LEARNED

The following lessons emerged from the operation of the project, and they are discussed in detail in turn:

- A new way of thinking
- The stress of the move
- Whose house?
- Home making
- Management of the vehicle
- Living in the community
- Communication systems
- Liaison
- Recruitment and training of support workers
- Sustaining enthusiasm and quality
- Supervision
- Power relationships
- Family involvement
- Representatives and advocates
- Management
- Accountability

A NEW WAY OF THINKING

For people like Kathy and Victoria to hold the tenancy of their own home was a very new concept for most people. It took time and much negotiation to get the idea across to the Housing Department, the utility companies and the banks and building societies. The parents found they needed to be very clear about what was needed, persistent and insistent. They never accepted no for an answer and saw the whole process as one of educating the various services. They insisted that there were no legal barriers to opening accounts with banks, building societies and the utilities; the various services just needed to get their heads around the idea and eventually they did.

There was a commitment to the idea of the project from the agency providing care support and its workers. It took some time to realise that while both management and support workers might feel committed to the concept of independent living, in practice they were failing to deliver the quality of service which would make this a reality.

There seemed to be three main reasons for this:

1. There was a failure to grasp the special nature of a profound learning disability. Hitherto the care agency had expected all its clients to play their part in directing their own care. The agency seemed unprepared to accept that people with the severe degree of learning disability experienced by Kathy, Victoria and Lisa, would never be able to do this in a direct sense. This was felt by the parents to be a failure to accept the reality of the severity of the learning disability, and therefore to set appropriate targets. They wondered if it was easier to accept that someone cannot see or walk as well as usual, than that someone cannot learn, think or communicate very easily.

2. The management structure of the agency was not sufficiently flexible to cope with this new dimension in their work. When women like Kathy, Victoria and Lisa are established in their own home, their directions for care have to be interpreted by those working with them. Unless this process includes families, friends and representatives as valid partners, big mistakes can be made by those who have not known the women for very long. At its worst an authoritarian approach can develop, enforcing the ideology of a manager or support worker, sometimes in the genuine belief that the parents or representatives are over-protective.

3. Social Services management structures for the project were not clear, especially with respect to their relationship with the care agency management. In particular, there were no clear systems for accountability, monitoring and review arrangements.

The key issues of management and representation/advocacy are discussed more fully later in the chapter. In general it is clear that the only way round this problem is a structured partnership involving parents/representatives with workers and managers in an on-going dialogue. No one has all the answers, but there must be respect for the experience and knowledge of family and friends, as well as a willingness to consider fresh approaches and new ideas from support workers keen to do their best for the women. The role of any manager at whatever level would then be to reinforce the systems developed by the women and their representatives.

THE STRESS OF THE MOVE

On reflection, the parents feel that they underestimated the effect of the move on Kathy and Victoria. So much energy was needed to take part in the planning procedures, make all the practical arrangements and cope with bureaucratic inefficiency and delays, that little was left over to consider this issue. They talked to the women about the move, made visits to the house before they moved in and involved them in shopping for goods. However, although it was seen by everyone as a move to a better situation, it did involve uprooting Kathy and Victoria from familiar if unsatisfactory arrangements and the staff they were used to, transfer to new GPs and paramedics, key figures in their lives, and the move to a new neighbourhood. In similar situations the parents would recommend:

1. It must be recognised that there will be a long lead-in period from the initial concept of the project to people moving in. This project opened comparatively quickly, less than two years after the first tentative discussions. Similar projects have taken more like five years from planning to completion. If new building rather than adaptations is necessary, the period may be even longer. Delays should be anticipated from causes outside the control of the planners, such as arrangements with outside contractors. This project moved fast for a number of reasons, including the enthusiasm and hard work of those involved in planning, but also because of the pressure resulting from the unsatisfactory care arrangements being experienced by Kathy and Victoria.

2. There must be a collaborative model of planning involving representatives of those taking up the tenancies including parents, social workers, occupational therapists, physiotherapists, social services officers, and the agency undertaking care arrangements. The planning group must insist that unilateral decisions by one party because of bureaucratic requirements must not be made as they could compromise the project. The planning arrangements for this project worked well in this respect. Difficult issues were raised openly in

meetings and everyone was involved in making what were sometimes
very hard decisions. Nevertheless, there is some very complex
communication, and wires can get crossed. At one stage decisions
about adaptations involved the architect, two occupational therapists,
two social workers, two sets of parents and the social services officer,
the latter with the unenviable task of obtaining permission for the
financial outlay through a labyrinth of social services senior
management and council committees.

3. A structured approach to the move should be adopted, with everyone
   concerned involved in discussion at every appropriate opportunity,
   using visual clues such as pictures and photographs. There are no easy
   answers. Kathy, for example, had never liked empty houses and on
   preliminary visits to the house became very distressed if she stayed for
   long, even with a favourite blanket and toys. If you did not know
   Kathy, you might have concluded that she had taken a dislike to the
   new house.

4. During and after the move there should be an agreed process to
   monitor and follow up the reactions of the women, in order to
   respond constructively to any adverse changes. This is not easy either.
   Kathy was quite unwell during this period so it was difficult to
   separate that from any uncertainties about her new situation. It
   probably comes down to more awareness and sensitivity by
   everybody in acknowledging the likely stress, and organised
   opportunities to share any concerns. As many people with profound
   intellectual and multiple disabilities will be quite frail, awareness of
   possible increased stress is particularly important as it may lead to a
   worsening of health. It is most important to review compatibility of
   tenants within three months, and there need to be back-up
   arrangements in case incompatibility occurs. In Victoria's case her
   place at her previous residential unit was kept open for a period, and
   the Social Services Department had confirmed that it would be
   responsible for making any arrangements for residential care should
   the project prove unviable, or unsuitable for either of the women.

WHOSE HOUSE?

There is no doubt that the house is Victoria's and Lisa's home. Their names
are on the tenancy agreement, and they own all the furniture and equipment.
They both know it is their home, recognise it and are glad to return there.

Their home reflects their interests and personalities in its furnishings, pictures and decorations.

Great emphasis and importance has always been placed by the parents and the agency's management on the fact that the house belongs to both women. In practice, this is not always fully realised by workers, some of whom use the women's household equipment such as the telephone inappropriately, or stick notices to walls with cellotape.

Workers need to be regularly supervised so that this principle is followed, and it is ensured that they understand they are not working in an institution. Induction and training must reinforce this essential principle.

HOME MAKING

Both women, through their representatives, set the standards of how their home should function. It should be a safe, warm, clean and pleasant place to live in, with comfortable furniture and good food; the atmosphere should be relaxed and calm. It should be a haven, a good place to return to, a welcome place for visitors and a place of which to be proud.

When recruiting workers, the criteria should include essential homemaking skills such as working to a domestic budget, cooking, taking care of clothes and personal possessions, small repairs and all domestic chores. All workers should be able to work as part of a team with a systematic approach to the women's agreed objectives.

MANAGEMENT OF THE VEHICLE

To ensure that the vehicle is used well, clear guidelines covering its maintenance, reports of accidents and standards of safety have been written by the parents. A clear annual budget for the vehicle is in the House Book. A log book is kept in the vehicle for staff to enter details for every journey.

To ensure this happens and staff follow the maintenance system, spot and regular checks need to be done by the manager. It is essential that workers are absolutely clear that the vehicle belongs to, and is for the sole use of, the women. These matters must be clearly understood and reinforced by the manager or a vehicle used by a number of workers may deteriorate rapidly, misuse of the vehicle may occur and simple repairs may be neglected, causing major expense.

LIVING IN THE COMMUNITY

In the light of experience a fine balance must be found so that all the people in the house feel secure and safe. Information must be given to all staff members about the nature and location of the surroundings of the house. Explicit details of the importance of the house's security must be made clear.

Members of staff must be innovative and imaginative to enable and encourage people with learning disabilities to participate in community life. They need to be aware of what issues are important to the people living on an estate or a street, and consider whether the women should join a tenants/residents association. The house should regularly take the local newspaper and workers should read the local library notices. The women should be enabled to join MENCAP and other organisations, so that they can join in events and be visible in their own community.

COMMUNICATION SYSTEMS

For communication to work well in such a house:

1. All workers including relief staff, must be made aware of the existence and use of the handbooks such as the care books, House book and the House and personal diaries, and their importance must be stressed by both representatives and management.

2. The use of the systems must be checked periodically by the manager, and their importance reinforced with workers.

At the outset of each shift the support worker should read entries in the personal and house diaries, so they are aware of changing circumstances, health problems, appointments and arrangements, and so on. If they are using the vehicle they should read the last entries in the log book and make their own entry as appropriate when the journey is completed. Before going off duty support workers should complete the personal diary for the period of their shift, and should also have recorded any telephone messages, appointments and other arrangements which have come to their attention during this time. If these things are done consistently, problems such as missed appointments, running out of supplies or medication and even misunderstandings about medical problems can be avoided.

The basis for these various systems is:

1. A service agreement between the representatives, care agency and funding authority, in this case the local authority.

2. An operational policy and practice which provides a framework for everyone involved to work to agreed objectives on behalf of the person involved.

The authors feel strongly that similarly detailed documents and procedures will be required in any independent living project providing for people with profound intellectual and multiple disabilities.

LIAISON

Both women have multiple disabilities and this means their health is vulnerable. Parents, from experience, know that unless great care and attention to detail is given to their health needs, deterioration can set in with surprising speed and very serious consequences may ensue.

The needs of people with multiple disabilities are by definition extremely complex, and require their representatives, workers and professionals to work in a collaborative manner. Representatives and some established workers know a good deal about the physical, emotional and psychological needs of the women, and this knowledge and expertise must be valued and utilised by professionals.

It is also important that different professionals such as the GP and the physiotherapist are enabled to work collaboratively on the medical and other needs of the women.

RECRUITMENT AND TRAINING OF SUPPORT WORKERS

Recruitment

The care agency had a policy of involving users in the recruitment of staff who would work with them. It was initially agreed that representatives of the women would be involved in this process but in practice this has not happened. When the women took up residence some of the workers were familiar to Kathy as they had worked with her in previous residential settings, and some had worked briefly with Victoria before she moved from her residential unit. Some important considerations have emerged from what has happened since:

1. Representatives of users with profound intellectual and multiple disabilities should be involved in initial and subsequent recruitment of support workers.

2. Ways must be found of bringing together observations about the reactions of people like Kathy, Victoria and Lisa to different members

of staff. If staff are on probationary periods, such observations along with the views of representatives should feed into the process of deciding whether such appointments should become permanent.

3. Managers have an important role in ensuring the selection of a balanced staff team. There should be a range of ages to ensure that there is plenty of useful experience, but also freshness and enthusiasm. Equal opportunities policies must take account of the needs of the disabled tenants. They should also apply to recruitment procedures, to ensure that workers are sensitive to the culture and background of those for whom they are providing care support. At least a proportion of staff should directly reflect this culture and background. Disabled women requiring intimate personal care may prefer to have all female workers.

4. Managers must be alert to changes in the staff team, ensuring that when vacancies are about to occur posts are advertised and filled promptly. If this is not done over-use of relief workers can occur and quality and standards can spiral rapidly downwards.

Induction

Induction should focus on the issues in the Operational Policy, and there should be a standard programme for all new staff with some shorter version for relief staff. The programme must include very practical sessions on care of the tenants and on managing the house. Representatives must be involved in the construction of any induction programme, to ensure that priority topics are included. They should also be directly involved in presentation of some parts of the programme, particularly in relating the family and personal history of the person with the disabilities, and in conveying personal preferences, interests, ways of communicating and ways in which life can be made rich and meaningful for the person they represent.

Without thorough induction bad habits can set in from the first shift, and anxiety on the part of staff can lead to misunderstandings with parents and representatives, and misinterpretations of the women's needs and wishes.

On-going training

On-going training is essential:

1. So that any anxieties or difficulties can be aired and addressed.

2. To keep up with new developments and ideas, learning from good practitioners.

3. To keep up with and share changes in the women's health, skills and personal development.

4. To enable interaction with other staff in what can be a lonely and isolating job; regular in-service training can be a powerful factor in maintaining staff morale.

For this training to be effective the following points need to be agreed:

1. Representatives should be involved in planning in-service training to ensure that full consideration is given to all topics which may need to be addressed.

2. It should be possible to tap into training arrangements provided locally by health and social services authorities if they are seen to be appropriate.

3. There must be an identified budget for in-service training and the person responsible for managing the project should produce an annual report to account for this.

SUSTAINING ENTHUSIASM AND QUALITY

Working with women like Kathy, Victoria and Lisa can be very rewarding and exciting. It can also be demanding and draining. Working alone for many hours with someone who does not communicate verbally can be a strain for all parties. The work can be hard physically. Good workers should not be left to burn themselves out. Some ideas to prevent this are:

1. The staff team manager should ensure that celebration of achievements by the disabled person is a regular part of team meetings. Workers should be enabled to feel proud that they have contributed to developments, and need to know that managers and other workers will support them in building on these. The parents found that workers were often bursting to tell them of some progress. However modest this was, it was important that it was recognised and taken up. These discussions should be based on the monitoring of personal development plans drawn up for and with the disabled person and her representatives.

2. Shift patterns need to be carefully structured. In such small scale projects it is convenient to allocate workers to long shifts to include sleep-ins. This can be very stressful for all parties and this stress and tiredness can lead to poor decision making.

3. A house with two disabled tenants is more like an ordinary home than
    one with four, six or more. However, the small scale brings an
    increased risk of isolation. A worker may be alone with one of the
    disabled tenants for many hours. While the individual needs of each
    disabled person need to be considered when planning the day's
    activities, it would seem sensible to encourage regular joint outings,
    social gatherings and shopping to take some of the intensity out of
    the one-to-one relationship.

4. Regular joint team meetings and regular in-service training will enable
    experiences to be shared and the further development of skills by the
    support workers. Meetings should also provide an opportunity to air
    the usual grumbles about some workers not doing their fair share of
    housework, or choosing only the more congenial activities. These
    grievances can fester in such an enclosed working environment if
    there is no opportunity to talk them through.

SUPERVISION

In the demanding job of support worker, regular supervision by a manager
is essential and should ensure:

1. That workers are supported in working to agreed goals and plans,
    referring to their individual job descriptions, the Operational Policy
    and the individual care plans. This will ensure accountability.

2. That support is given to workers in resolving anxieties and difficulties
    and in experiencing feelings of anger, pain at the nature of the
    disability or if the disabled person dies, resentment of other staff and
    similar issues.

3. That help is given to identify and clarify the many problems which
    may arise in the course of the work.

4. That staff are using and developing their skills and strengths, and that
    training needs are identified and met.

5. That the project has control over staff.

6. That inappropriate staff attitudes are addressed and corrected.

For supervision to be effective the following must apply:

1. Supervision needs to be a priority, and sessions should only be
    cancelled in the direst emergency.

2. Supervision should be based on the current agreement about the aims
   of the project. The person supervising must be fully aware of the
   issues involved in the job, and should be a regular visitor to assess the
   care situation for themselves.

3. Managers, whether of staff or of the project, should also be given
   regular supervision sessions at an appropriate level.

POWER RELATIONSHIPS

People with any degree of learning disability are vulnerable to the power
and authority of others; people with profound intellectual and multiple
disabilities are among the most vulnerable in our society. They are totally
dependent on the people working with them; because of their profound
learning disabilities they cannot tell what has happened, indicate that
anything is amiss or fight back. This power can be exercised to the detriment
of those with disabilities by anyone who has control over aspects of their
lives – parents, other carers, professionals dealing with them. It can result in
over-protection, or manipulation and exploitation. There are, sadly, many
recorded examples, from earlier historical periods when disabled people were
neglected, mocked and abused, to more recent times with repeated scandals
in long stay hospitals and other residential units.

The parents of Kathy and Victoria had experienced the neglect of their
daughters in residential units. Kathy was in hospital for three months after
her parents removed her from her first residential placement, with dysentery,
bed sores, malnutrition and the effects of inappropriate medication. Victoria
suffered pain, discomfort and loss of mobility when she did not receive
regular physiotherapy. This was one of the main reasons the parents wanted
their daughters to be as near the family home as possible, so that frequent
visiting was possible. It was also a reason for insisting on open practices,
with parental involvement in planning, monitoring and evaluating services.

It is essential that all who work with this vulnerable group are aware of
the potential for exercising power. It may be something affecting everyday
life such as making someone wait for a meal, insisting that a drink can only
be taken at the end of a meal or removing a favourite activity; it may involve
actions affecting relationships, such as resisting the involvement of parents
and friends because of a feeling that young people should be completely
independent of their families. Apparently trivial or more important, practical
or emotional, the exercise of power without thinking through the implications can be very destructive to those with disabilities.

Most recorded abuses have taken place in institutional settings. As independent living is still relatively rare for people with profound intellectual and multiple disabilities, it is worth considering what safeguards can be put in place to guarantee their rights.

1. There should be regular sharing of information on the communication methods of those with disabilities by all those involved with their care. A meeting to discuss this, say every three months, would help new workers and would avoid the situation where a particular worker may be misinterpreting attempts at communication, or may, perhaps unwittingly, be introducing their own ideas about what should be happening without fully considering the wishes of those with the disabilities. It has been the experience of the parents that their daughters will go on trying valiantly to express their wishes and feelings, despite many frustrating responses. Crying and other expressions of distress can otherwise be misinterpreted as challenging behaviour, when the women may be trying to convey physical pain, or the lack of a favoured activity, or deep feelings. Kathy's parents remember her being very angry on one occasion, and brushing aside all attempts at comfort. They were very worried that she might be in terrible pain as the screams rose higher; eventually it turned out that she wanted one particular book to look at, and once they had sorted out which one, she calmed down. When people have no verbal communication and have difficulty in making sense of the world, they have to exaggerate the forms of communication they do possess, to be taken notice of. Regular dialogue amongst all those concerned can also lead to suggestions for developing the communication skills of the person with disabilities, and improving awareness of the various methods they use by anyone working with them.

2. All those working on a project like this must accept the basic rights of the disabled person as set out in the Operational Policy. However, this acceptance must be seen to be translated into practice. Regular monitoring of day-to-day routines, interactions and decision making must be undertaken by those managing the project. Discussion of these matters should take place through supervision and through staff team meetings. Representatives of the disabled person must have a place in this process, and the right to raise questions about what is taking place.

3. One fear parents of people with profound intellectual and multiple disabilities have is that their son or daughter will be physically, sexually or emotionally abused. Who would know? Trust in support workers can only be enhanced if there is an atmosphere of open discussion about the project, and representatives are fully involved in such discussion. Managers have a difficult and delicate task in handling situations where one worker might have suspicions of another. There should be clear procedures for workers and representatives to report such suspicions, and for matters to be followed through.

4. One issue faced straight away by the parents was whether a male member of staff should be recruited to the team. One family at first agreed to this after much consideration, but the other family felt this was not an option for their daughter. Where intimate personal care will be given, much consideration and consultation will be needed before appointing support workers of another gender. Representatives should have a right of veto if they have any doubts.

FAMILY INVOLVEMENT

The recognition, awareness and importance of what family means to someone with a learning disability must never be underestimated or denied. Distant family members, although not in regular contact, may want to be involved in their relative's life. Family ties and links need working on, first to achieve, and then to maintain them. The family's culture and values should be taken into consideration as they influence the care package.

Important life events such as a birthday or anniversary must always be acknowledged on the day, and workers should enable the person with a learning disability to celebrate positively. Workers will also need to know important dates for the family, and facilitate the posting of cards and buying of presents. Workers should be aware of, and follow, the family's traditions – family meals at festival times, barbecue suppers in the summer, going with the family to joint community events such as barn dances and summer fairs.

When parents or representatives visit a disabled person in their own home, they may be going in several capacities. They will visit as a friend to socialise, chat, laugh, have a cuddle; they may bring items for the house; they may come to do some work in the garden; they may be helping new support workers with some of the care routines; they may visit if the disabled person is sick; they may come to sort out bills or other financial matters; they may come to check up on something.

Expectations about family involvement need to be made clear at the outset if misunderstandings on both sides are to be avoided.

In this project, due to the absence of designated social workers for long periods, family members had no choice but to take on various roles which in other circumstances may have been carried out by care managers and advocates. When there were more difficulties with matters not being followed through, and when the women's health was seen to be at risk, they had to step in and sort matters out.

REPRESENTATIVES AND ADVOCATES

At an early stage in the planning process for the project, the group discussed who would represent the needs and wishes of the women to those organising and giving care support. It became clear during further discussions that there were no easy answers. The parents accepted that at some stage, if the project was to be independent of them, there would need to be others who were authorised to represent the needs and wishes of the women.

There are two main reasons why people with profound intellectual and multiple disabilities should have independent representatives/advocates:

1. The parents may die before the disabled person and her interests will need to be safeguarded by someone else.

2. It will enable the growth of all possible independence for the disabled person.

Representatives may include parents, siblings, other relatives, friends, or independent advocates.

Parents need to know who will be looking out for their son or daughter when they are no longer there. Establishing an independent representative or advocate for their daughter can be seen as an investment for their future.

Who is qualified and authorised to act as an advocate, to interpret and express the needs of someone with profound intellectual and multiple disabilities? What is the job specification, and how much time will they be expected to give?

Knowledge and experience would seem to be the pre-requisites for acting as an advocate:

1. Knowledge of the person.

2. Knowledge of their disabilities and any medical conditions.

3. Knowledge and experience of their care routines.

4. Knowledge of their history.

5. Knowledge of the context within which they live.

6. Knowledge of their social links – family, friends.

7. Knowledge of their interests – leisure, cultural.

8. Knowledge and experience of how they communicate their wishes and needs.

It is also important to ask who is benefiting from this relationship.

Difficulty of recruiting and retaining advocates

Advocacy for people like Kathy, Victoria and Lisa is still in its development stage. There is experience but it is not widespread. Advocates need to be recruited, trained and then supported by an agency independent of the funding and providing agencies, parents and family; money is needed by voluntary groups to do this. Advocates need to be very committed; their role must be clearly defined, as it must not be confused with management functions. It is unrealistic to expect advocates to stay for many years. Realistically, disabled people must expect new advocates every year or two, just as they have learned to accept frequent changes in support workers. Advocates will not necessarily be readily found, and replacements may not be found in time to dovetail when one leaves. In such periods of transition it will usually fall to the family to fill the gap.

Being an advocate for someone with profound intellectual and multiple disabilities is very challenging. Parents have sometimes introduced potential advocates to their daughter, only to find they are unable to cope with the lack of verbal communication, the physical disabilities, the medical problems and the unpredictable behaviour. Building a relationship with someone like Kathy, Victoria or Lisa is a slow process. The setting needs to ensure that both parties feel comfortable and relaxed. The expectations and aims of the relationship need to be clearly set out at the start. An advocate would need to do a good deal of reading to learn about the disabled person and to meet members of the family and friends. The boundaries of the role should be clearly defined so there is no confusion or overlap with managers, social workers, family, friends and others; the advocate would however need to relate to and work with all these people. Any advocate in this situation would need the backing of an organisation which could offer training and regular support. Managers of the project should recognise the importance of, and foster any burgeoning relationship – the women's workers should welcome and assist any potential advocate and see this as part of their job.

It is the manager's role in projects like this to co-ordinate the many actions needed to ensure that people like Kathy, Victoria and Lisa are happy, comfortable and safe. The advocate should be aware of any problems and have an agreed channel to raise these; they would also interpret and represent wishes on such matters as changes in activities, changes in lifestyle, the development of relationships, spending of any surplus money, and look at changing needs such as health, new skills, leisure, changes in funding of care support, bereavement.

The relationship between managers, advocates and other representatives must be a partnership, not an imposition. Long experience and knowledge of the disabled person must be balanced by fresh approaches and a willingness to experiment to extend independence. However proven and necessary care routines, such as the use of particular toiletries for bathing and washing to prevent skin problems, must not be discarded in this process, through thoughtlessness, carelessness or misguided ideas about representatives. This partnership must be formalised in the Operational Policy and in regular structured contact; it will, however, only live and breathe if all concerned want it to work, and realise that this will be in the best interests of the disabled person.

It must be recognised that the question of advocacy for people with profound intellectual and multiple disabilities is extremely complex. Many people with learning disabilities can, with support, express their feelings and wishes. Profound intellectual and multiple disability does not just mean communicating is more difficult, it means that person takes more time and has more difficulty in formulating those wishes and feelings. This is an essential feature of the disability and cannot be ignored.

In this project the questions of representation and advocacy are still under discussion. In the meantime the parents, their families and friends form a network of representatives for each of the women.

MANAGEMENT

It is of paramount importance that good management structures and procedures are set up and written down before a project like this becomes operational. Although procedures and even structures can, and indeed should, be changed in response to lessons learned once the project is underway, it is essential that the process for making changes is also written down and is clear to all those involved in the project. It can be all too easy once the initial euphoria is dispersed for bad practice to creep in and for changes to be made without any management sanction.

The requirements of good management are explicit lines of accountability, regular and skilful supervision, consistent training for all workers, written guidelines of good practice, written grievance and disciplinary procedures and written recruitment procedures. All the procedures should be in accordance with an equal opportunities policy.

All parties involved in setting up this project would probably agree that its momentum outran existing procedures and mechanisms, especially with respect to the role of the local authority. The authors feel this is the root cause of most of the difficulties which have arisen.

ACCOUNTABILITY

However small the project, its accountability to those with particular interest in it must be explicit. There will generally be four elements to this:

- clients
- parents, other family members, other representatives
- the management committee
- the funding body.

Ways in which the clients' interests can be represented must be carefully thought through. In many instances, the parents will be the best representative of their sons or daughters. If independent advocates are available locally, they may have a key role, either as sole representatives or in partnership with the family.

A management or executive committee should be set up to bring together all interests such as the funding agency, the care manager, the care agency, the family, advocates and the clients. This may be a sub-committee formed from the committee of a charity responsible for staffing the project, or a body set up by the local social services or health authority representing the various interests. The management committee would have responsibility for deciding the overall policies of the project, such as how new tenants are selected, ensuring the quality of its service and agreeing the operational policy.

The care manager would be responsible for convening regular meetings of workers, representatives, OTs, physiotherapists, and any other relevant individuals, to discuss day to day issues, for example the monitoring and up-dating of personal development plans.

Accountability to the funding body will normally be achieved through compliance with a written contract. The funding body, which may be the local social services department or the health authority or a combination of both, and may also include other bodies such as charitable trusts, should monitor and evaluate the performance of the care agency. The procedure to be used to do this should be clearly set out in the contract. Failure on the part of the agency to meet the required standards should be addressed as soon as this is identified. The funding body may insist on additional staff training or supervision, or may alter the contract in other ways. If the agency is unable to meet the contracts specification the funding body may decide to close the contract and award it to another agency.

At the time of writing, the purchasing functions of social services departments are still relatively new, and may not be fully operational or well developed in all areas.

In order that the interests of the clients are addressed it is important that each is allocated someone with responsibility for reviewing the service regularly and monitoring how effective it is for the client. This person may be a social worker or may be a care manager, appointed from any of a number of professional staff. The care manager should be located on the purchasing side of the funding agency so that s/he holds responsibility for buying the service and for monitoring the contract. The care manager will have dual interest, ensuring the highest possible quality of life for the client and also the best value for money for the purchaser. The role of the care manager must be clearly defined.

One of the difficulties of a project like that for Kathy, Victoria and Lisa is that the care agency may treat it as 'belonging' to the agency rather than to the clients. Thus the project may be perceived as an institution. The principle that the project belongs to the two women, who are buying much of the service with money received directly from the Independent Living Fund is a fundamental one.

CONCLUSION

In Chapter 10 a number of recommendations have been made. This conclusion does not set out to simply repeat or summarise those recommendations, but looks back over the material covered by the book and highlights some key lessons.

The parents had always argued that if you could get services right for people with complex disabilities like Kathy and Victoria, it should be relatively easy to set up appropriate services for people with less severe disabilities.

This was the reverse of what they had always been told when, for example in the 1970s, the local authority said their daughters were too severely handicapped to be in a local residential facility, and again in 1984 when Kathy's parents were told that as she now had to use a naso-gastric tube permanently, she should go to a long stay hospital.

It is perhaps a positive sign of changing thinking that when Pat and Jean began to formulate the idea of Kathy and Victoria living in their own home, this time they received help and encouragement from the local authority Principal Officer for Learning Difficulties. He too took the view that the success of this project should show the way for others.

It is also important to emphasise that this project costs the local authority about half of the cost of caring for someone like Kathy, Victoria or Lisa in a local authority residential unit, private or voluntary home, because of the Independent Living Fund contribution to care costs. A relatively small increase in expenditure on more effective management and training would help to deal with some of the problems raised earlier.

The key issues of good communication, effective liaison, a balanced staff team, good quality and on-going training, definition of roles, management and accountability have been discussed in detail. All these, especially the crucial ones of management and accountability, are being explored by all parties concerned with the project at Kendal House, with the aim of creating more effective mechanisms for dealing with difficulties and evaluating success.

Equal status between purchasers and providers is essential if the project is to succeed in the long term. In a project like this, this means equal status for those representing the purchasers, in this case Kathy, Victoria and Lisa, who are unable to do this directly themselves.

If this equal status is really accepted by all parties, it makes it easier to deal with things that go wrong before a real crisis erupts. Parents and other representatives need to be able to voice concerns and even criticism without fear of repercussions, either for them in terms of their relationship with managers, workers and their son or daughter, or for their son or daughter directly in the quality of service they are offered. There has been good reason for such fears in long stay hospitals and other residential settings. Now complaints procedures should be in place and advertised in every residential setting, but old managerial attitudes still survive and there can be a tendency for the procedure to favour the institution and the workers, and to penalise the resident and their representatives, however unintentional this may be.

Above all, such a project succeeds when it provides meaningful choices for people like Kathy, Victoria and Lisa. Ways of interpreting and translating those perceived wishes must be constantly sought, so that the young women are genuinely involved in developing their capacity to choose and initiate, in areas such as food, clothes and daily routines, as well as in more complex areas such as relationships. This and not just a better quality of 'care' is what will make the opportunities offered by an independent living project such as this so different from other options.

The authors felt it was important to analyse the lessons learned in some detail, to offer guidance for others involved in setting up similar projects. The process should also help the project at Kendal House to move forward. Despite the various problems which have been discussed, it is vital to stress that this project has provided the young women involved with unprece-dented opportunities for personal development. The one-to-one relationship with their support workers offers the possibility of continuing learning and development of skills and interests in a way which would just not have been possible in their previous residential settings. Above all, they are living in their own home, at last.

The Care Package

The agency chosen to provide support workers was involved from the very beginning of the planning process.

The details of the care package were arrived at after a full discussion of the needs of the two women, which were identified as follows:

1. They were totally dependent on others for all physical care, preparation of food, giving of medication, etc.

2. Their profound learning disabilities meant they could not direct their care or the running of the household.

3. Either might have a medical emergency at any time.

4. Neither had any sense of danger.

5. They could not be left alone in the house for even a few moments, because of the above considerations.

6. Nevertheless, both women had many interests and enjoyed outings and varied activities, including spending time with family and friends.

The final agreed care hours

Kathy	16 hours per day
Victoria	16 hours per day
	and a shared sleep-in of 8 hours.

(Budgeted for 365 days of the year).

Total cost of the care package (April 1991)

Total care costs	£97,580.00 (per annum)
ILF maximum grant	£41,600.00
Islington Council	£55,980.00

Points to note

1. Islington Social Services made it clear from the outset that their contribution to care costs must not exceed the amount they were currently paying for Kathy and Victoria; they would prefer to make a saving.

2. As a result this package was pared down to the minimum felt to be workable. Originally it was planned that there would be two workers for Victoria at the busiest times such as getting up in the morning, and two workers sleeping in.

3. The ILF grant was the maximum for London, but the total given included the whole of the Severe Disability Premium and half of the amount of Attendance Allowance (now Disability Living Allowance, care component, highest rate) received by the women, and which they were expected to contribute to care costs.

4. The costs would cover staffing for 365 days of the year, ie. the maximum projected costs. The intention behind this was to allow for all eventualities such as illness of the women requiring one of them to stay in the house, day centres or other planned activities being closed, hospital appointments, unforeseen circumstances leading to cancellation of a planned stay with parents, etc.

5. Kathy's and Victoria's workers were organised as separate teams. They shared the sleep-in worker who might be from either team, and workers from one team could cover for a sick member of the other team. In practice they needed to work together closely to ensure the harmonious running of the house.

6. If cover for sickness could not be provided by regular staff, relief staff from a commercial agency would be used. Every effort would be made to use a small pool of such staff who would therefore get to know the women. However, the Operational Policy and care guidelines had to be sufficiently clear and detailed to enable a worker who had never met the women before to care for them successfully.

7. Induction would always take place with regular staff new to the project. However, after the project had started it became clear that there was no identified budget for in-service training. The care agency said this had to be funded from any underspend on care costs or from bank interest.

Comparable costs

Informal inquiries during 1993 produced rough figures as annual costings in the following types of residential establishments, for someone with profound intellectual and multiple disabilities, excluding costs for any day provision:

A. A long-stay hospital place	£55,000
B. A local authority unit	£55,000
C. A voluntary home	£55,000

Good quality care for someone with profound intellectual and multiple disabilities is never going to be cheap. It is interesting that the independent living option is not as expensive as institutional alternatives. Even if costings are added in for regular in-service training and overall management, as we would recommend for the future, the costings are still comparable.

Operational Policy and Practice for The Home of Katherine Sirockin and Victoria Willson

CONTENTS

1. Philosophy and Aims
2. Exclusions
3. Organisation and Management
4. Staff Organisation
5. Training Policy
6. Supplies/Storage/Disposal
7. Fire and Safety
8. Budget Policy
9. Transport
10. Privacy of Clients/Visitors Policy
11. Communication
12. Monitoring and Evaluation
13. Medical Care
14. Issues of Sexuality
15. Unforeseen problems

Appendices

1. Islington Council Social Services Policy Statement on People with Learning Disabilities
2. Service Agreement between Islington Council, Katherine Sirockin, Victoria Willson and (name of care agency)
3. Care Agency – User Guidelines
4. Workers' Guidelines
5. Job Description
6. Complaints Procedure
7. Health and Safety
8. Daily tasks for both women,
   Weekly tasks,
   Monthly tasks,
   Annual tasks.
9. Emergencies

NOTE: The Operational Policy and Practice should be adhered to in conjunction with Appendices 1 to 9.

Pat Fitton, Jean Willson, 1991.

Only Appendices 1, 2, 8 and 9 are reproduced. Appendices 3 to 7 are specific to the practices of one care contractor.

1.0 Philosophy, aims and equal opportunities

1.1   Our starting point is the LBI Social Services Policy Statement on People with Learning Difficulties, 11.1.91 (Appendix B1).

1.2   All have a need and a right to a place to live.

1.3   This house will provide a home for these two women as long as they need and want to live there.

1.4   It will enable both women to live as independently as possible in a home of their own.

1.5   It will enable both women to realise their full potential in all aspects of their lives, including all possible self-determination. For self-determination to be a reality it is recognised that it will be necessary for support workers to find ways to actively seek the women's choice. Careful observation of the women's own communication and response by all involved in the project is essential, so that this can be understood, represented and promoted. Planning imaginative ways to enable the women to actively participate in their daily living is important. Training in this area as well as support from others eg. OT, is a priority.

1.6   Support/care will be provided by (name of care agency) (see Service Agreement Appendix B2).

1.7   All involved in the project will recognise the special requirements resulting from the severe learning disability of each woman, and their consequent inability to direct their care and household and other arrangements. All will agree to adopt an approach of sharing information, expertise, training, etc. in the interests of delivering a coherent and effective support service to these women. Specific arrangements for this will be decided in discussion involving care agency management, support workers, representatives of the women, social workers and specialist workers as appropriate, eg. OTs, physiotherapists, etc. These arrangements may be considered for revision from time to time at the suggestion of any party.

1.8 EQUAL OPPORTUNITIES
    A commitment to equal opportunities regardless of race, gender, social class or disability underpins all aspects of this policy and practice. This refers to matters specifically affecting the two women, to management and staffing policies, and to all operational matters.

1.9 RISK TAKING
    Every attempt will be made to open up opportunities for activity and development of the two women. This will be balanced by an awareness of their vulnerability arising from their multiple disabilities.

1.10 The philosophy serves to promote the best interests of the two women and is backed by detailed guidelines contained in or attached to this document. See also Appendix B.

2.0 Exclusions

2.1   Both women, with advice should they wish it from appropriate representatives and support workers, will decide who is and is not allowed in the home.

2.2   Should either of the women choose or need to move, the other woman and her representatives will be fully involved in decisions about any replacement.

3.0 Organisation and management

3.1   Co-ordination and service specifications – role of contractor: all support staff will follow the care agency Guidelines and Job Guidelines. See Appendices B4 and B5.

3.2   Overall management structures for the project – to be decided with the London Borough of Islington.

3.3   All parties are working towards achieving independent representatives/advocates for the two women.

4.0 Staff organisation

4.1   It is agreed that care be provided for 24 hours per day.

4.2   (Name of care agency) will provide an agreed number of workers whose role is to carry out all tasks agreed between the women's representatives and care agency management, by following explicit directions provided, usually in writing by the representatives.

4.3   (Name of care agency) are the employers. All workers are required to work to care agency Guidelines at all times.

4.4   Workers will be recruited following care agency Equal Opportunities procedure, paying specific regard to skills necessary to work with Katherine Sirockin and Victoria Willson. The two women, and their representatives, will be included in the recruitment process of their workers.

4.5   It is (name of care agency) responsibility to ensure that Katherine Sirockin and Victoria Willson have assistance at the agreed times and that in so far as it is possible, continuity of support is safe-guarded. Shifts are organised according to the needs and wishes of the user. Details of current shift rotas will be available in the house for the information of all concerned with the project.

4.6   (Name of care agency) will keep representatives up to date with any changes to the staff team.

4.7   Should there be disharmony, users and representatives will follow the care agency Complaints Procedure, Appendix B6.

5.0 Training policy

5.1   All new staff will receive a planned programme of training in all specific care tasks required by the two women before taking full responsibility for either or both. This training will comprise input from the women's representatives, care agency management, support workers and any other workers involved directly with the women, felt to be appropriate at that time. This initial training will be organised and structured by the care agency.

5.2   It is accepted that much on-going training will be of a less formal nature and will involve representatives and support workers working alongside one another and sharing experiences and views.

5.3   It is nevertheless accepted that periodically more formal and structured training should take place to remind and update support workers. This may involve outside agencies, other professional workers such as physiotherapists, etc. Representatives may make suggestions for and be involved in this training.

5.4 RELIEF STAFF

When it is necessary to use such staff on shifts, every effort will be made to use a small number of staff who will become familiar with the needs of the two women. If a relief worker new to either of the two women is going to be responsible for sole care of one or both women, every effort must be made to notify representatives so that they may exercise the option of going in to meet and possibly work with such a relief worker.

6.0 Supplies/storage/disposal

6.1   It will be the responsibility of support workers to ensure that all supplies are kept at an adequate level. This includes cleaning materials, toiletries, basic household items, incontinence supplies and medication. (Details of medication procedures will be found in Section 13.) This may involve shopping, ordering and liaising with appropriate agencies. Details of how to carry out these tasks and contact details for agencies will be found in the House Book.

6.2   Storage of supplies will be organised so that they are readily accessible and easily checked. Supplies will be kept in storage areas.

6.3   Disposal of waste, especially incontinence nappies and pads, should be
      immediate and with regard to basic hygiene and health precautions.
      Details of how to carry out these tasks will be found in the House Book.

7.0 Fire and safety

7.1   It is the responsibility of each and every support worker to ensure safe
      practices are followed to minimise fire risk and to carry out the
      evacuation of the women immediately should there be any suspicion of
      smoke and/or fire. Details of fire precautions and evacuation procedures
      are in the House Book.

7.2   It is the responsibility of support workers coming on duty to check they
      are aware of fire safety precautions/equipment eg. smoke detectors, fire
      blanket, and to check that window keys are readily accessible for each
      room.

7.3   At night when the front door is locked the support worker on duty will
      ensure they have the door keys with them at all times including in the
      sleeping in room.

7.4   Wheelchairs must be kept at the end of the bed to be readily accessible
      when either woman is in bed.

7.5   Workers will follow the care agency Health and Safety Policy, Appendix
      B7.

8.0 Budget policy – overall responsibility

8.1   Rigorous management of the finances of Katherine and Victoria is essential
      if the project is to be viable.

8.2   Workers will assist both women in collecting weekly benefits, with
      authorised signatures from their representatives. Benefits will be paid into
      their bank accounts. See House Book for procedure.

8.3   Weekly expenditure: staff will be responsible for keeping within the budget
      by following agreed procedures.

8.4   Periodic expenditure: clothing, personal items and holidays will be
      budgeted for individually. Further details will follow experience and
      discussion amongst all concerned.

8.5   Stationery for administration.
      Keep minor items eg. pens in stock from household kitty. Large and
      occasional items eg. diaries, record books, will be purchased individually
      or jointly from personal kitties. Always have stocks of pens.

8.6   Accounting.
      Workers will be responsible for monitoring all household and personal

accounts, by following the agreed procedures. Payment of all other bills eg. electricity – see procedures in House Book.

A separate file will be kept for each category:

- Electricity
- Gas
- Insurance
- Occasional bills eg. repairs
- Telephone
- Water.

8.7   Insurance: household contents. Claim for any loss or damage.

8.8   Workers must alert the care agency or the representatives if there appear to be financial difficulties.

8.9   Katherine and Victoria will each have two accounts.
One will be a building society account which receives ILF payments and issues payments to the care agency. Staff are to be aware of these accounts and to keep documentation safely, but will not be involved in transactions. The other account will be an account each for their benefits and expenditure:

> Victoria: Premium Account; TSB; 272 Upper Street, London N1.
>
> Katherine: Halifax Building Society; Upper Street, London N1.

Staff will be involved in deposits and withdrawals and will need to keep all documentation safely.

Katherine and Victoria also have a joint account for bills which will be administered by their representatives.

9.0 Transport policy

9.1   Staff will arrange regular outings to enable the two women to participate in activities they each enjoy. When transport is required, use will be made of the most economical form of transport as long as it is appropriate eg. London Taxi Card Scheme, Dial-a-Ride, etc.

9.2   Support workers will periodically check the validity of Taxi Cards, membership of Dial-a-Ride, etc. and renew if necessary.

9.3   Support workers will recognise that although the mobility allowance is intended to facilitate transport needs, it will not go very far if used on full price taxi rides. Special outings needing such provision will be planned in advance and budgeted for by lower expenditure during the next period.

9.4   When it is essential that one or both of the women keep an appointment, and a London scheme taxi or Dial-a-Ride cannot be arranged or fails, then a full price taxi should be used with lower expenditure budgeted for in the next two weeks to compensate.

9.5   Where longer journeys are planned eg. day trips or holidays, support workers will check out all access facilities thoroughly and ensure any necessary assistance is organised. Detailed check list is in the House Book.

9.6   Whatever form of transport is used, support workers will ensure that wheelchairs and wheelchair accessories are looked after at all stages of the journey.

9.7   Whatever form of transport is used, support workers will be responsible for ensuring the security, comfort and safety of the women during a journey. This will include ensuring any necessary seat belts or other restraints are correctly used. If either of the women is travelling in her wheelchair, the support worker is responsible for ensuring this is properly secured during the journey.

10.0 Visitor/privacy of clients policy

10.1   All involved in the project affirm that the house is first and foremost the home of the two women.

10.2   Any family member, friend or other representative visiting will usually phone or inform before an actual visit, and defer the visit if other plans have already been made.

10.3   No one will be invited to visit the house for the purpose of learning about the project without prior consultation with the women's representatives and workers. Such visits will be kept to a minimum.

10.4   Social workers, physiotherapists and all other professionals will make arrangements for visits in advance. These will be noted in the communication book.

10.5   All visitors not known to support workers, including people like meter readers, service workers, etc. will be required to give proof of identity and purpose of visit. If in doubt, support workers should ask the person to remain outside while they telephone for identification.

10.6   Children from the estate and locality should never be invited into the house.

10.7   All befrienders, etc. should be introduced to support workers and carry some form of authorisation when visiting or taking the women out.

10.8   Visitors to one woman may be asked to leave a particular room if she or the other woman needs personal attention.

10.9 Workers will agree with visitors on their arrival whether or not to remain in the room to provide assistance as and when required. The worker will remain within hearing distance.

10.10 Support workers will enable and encourage visiting and friendships for both women.

10.11 Support workers will organise return visits with friends and family where appropriate.

10.12 All concerned will recognise the vulnerability of both women in the following areas – physical, emotional, sexual, verbal and financial. Where workers feel anxious or uneasy about a visitor's conduct towards either woman, they will immediately contact the women's representatives and the care agency. If the worker considers the situation to be dangerous, they should contact the police immediately.

11.0 Communication

11.1 Clear communication is essential if the project is to work. It is the duty of everybody involved to take equal responsibility for explaining clearly, and making sure that what is said or written is understood.

11.2 The acknowledged representative(s) will provide the necessary directions/instructions in the women's stead. These will be simple, clear and precise. The workers' responsibility is to follow the directions provided. Workers close to Katherine and Victoria will be aware of their changing moods, likes, dislikes, health, strengths and needs, and will adapt directions accordingly.

Close observation of the women's non-verbal and verbal communication is essential. It is the role of the support workers to seek the women's views as far as possible eg. what food they want to eat, what clothes they want to wear, what to do, etc. In an attempt to elicit a choice or decision the support worker will need to offer a range of visual options and actual experience. It is important for each women's team of support workers to meet together regularly in order to share their observations so that a fuller picture of the women's likes, dislikes and preferences on a whole range of issues can be formed. These observations will be conveyed to the representatives. As observations are made, decisions will take place between representatives and workers as to any changes in direction, acknowledging that Katherine and Victoria each has the capacity to change their life style.

11.3 PLANNING FOR INDIVIDUAL NEEDS: PIN PROGRAMMES

These will be drawn up in full consultation with representatives and all carers. These will be reviewed initially every three months and thereafter every six months.

Those involved in planning will be:-

- Users
- Parents/Representatives
- Support workers and manager
- Day Centre or Service representatives
- Occupational Therapist
- Physiotherapist
- Medical advisers
- Social workers.

11.4 PERSONAL AND DOMESTIC CARE

All personal and domestic care tasks will be detailed in the Care Books and the House Book. These are to be kept up to date by the representatives and are kept in the house. An additional copy of each will be held in the care agency office. Any changes will be communicated verbally and confirmed in personal diaries and the Communication Book. ALL workers will follow these instructions at ALL times. The care agency manager will check frequently that this is being done, through individual supervision, team meetings and staff meetings.

11.5 COMMUNICATION WITHIN THE HOUSE

This will be by means of the House Diary and personal diaries for Katherine and Victoria. These must be consulted by all workers as soon as they come on duty. Support workers will carry out necessary recording during their period of duty. Comments should always be precise and give full details where appropriate eg. with hospital appointments, who is to go, transport arrangements made, etc. Methodical and clear recording should be made of all fits, bowel movements, fluid intake, exercises and outings in the personal diary.

11.6 COMMUNICATION BETWEEN THE WOMEN'S REPRESENTATIVES AND THE MANAGER

Regular meetings are to be held by the care agency management with the workers. Representatives may ask for issues to be discussed at these meetings. Scheduled attendance of parents/representatives will be every two months at team meetings. Representatives will meet the manager on a regular basis. Meetings may be arranged as and when required if there are issues of serious concern.

11.7 HANDOVER

There will be a formal handover between workers at every shift. Should a worker not turn up for the next shift, then it is the responsibility of the support worker on duty to inform the manager that they have failed to report. They must stay with the women until a replacement support worker arrives. Handover must then be given to this replacement worker. If a support worker for either woman does not come on duty in the morning it will be the responsibility of the worker sleeping-in to inform the manager. The sleep-in worker will continue to take responsibility, for both women if necessary, until a replacement worker arrives. Handover must then be given to this replacement worker.

11.8 HOUSEHOLD ARRANGEMENTS – REPAIRS, ETC.

Support workers will report problems eg. heating breakdown, to the appropriate agency as soon as the problem occurs. They will note arrangements made for repair, servicing, etc. and will outline those arrangements at handover, and will facilitate entry of service workers, etc. They will assist those on legitimate business eg. meter readers in locating meters, service workers in locating appliances, etc. (See House Book.) Service agreements are in operation for the washing machine, tumble drier and fridge/freezer. (See House Book for details of service agencies.)

12.0 Monitoring and evaluation

Representatives, Social Services and the care agency will be involved in this process. Details of procedures will follow further discussions amongst all those involved.

13.0 Medical care

13.1 Support workers are responsible for monitoring the health of the two women on a daily basis. This includes noting bruises, rashes, coughs, colds, abnormal temperatures and fit activity, and reporting to parents/representatives for direction. It will also include carrying out routine treatments eg. using arnica for bruises. See Care Books for instructions.

This responsibility may include arranging an appointment with the GP, asking for a GP visit, taking either woman to hospital casualty, calling an ambulance.

13.2 EPILEPTIC FITS

Detailed guidance on dealing with fit activity for Katherine and Victoria will be found in their individual Care Books. A summary is included in Appendix 2, Tasks.

13.3 EMERGENCIES

If the worker deems an emergency has arisen, they should call an ambulance immediately; they should then inform the care agency. Priority must be given to the woman experiencing the emergency even if this means a delay in informing the care agency.

If either woman is taken to hospital, the family and other designated representatives should be informed at the earliest opportunity by either the worker or the care agency.

In an emergency, it would be expected that the support worker for the other woman would offer assistance in whatever way possible, if they were present at the time, as long as this action was not going to place that woman at unacceptable risk.

13.4 Any medical appointments should be noted in the women's personal diaries and in the Communication Book. Staff coming on duty should check that arrangements have been made to keep those appointments.

13.5 Routine medication will be given to both women in accordance with agreed guidelines. Medication, dosage and administration details are kept in each bedroom.

13.6 Workers will be responsible for ensuring that adequate supplies of medication are available at all times. Procedures in the House Book should be followed.

14.0 Issues of sexuality

14.1 It is accepted by all involved with the project that both women will have sexual feelings and awareness.

14.2 Support workers will be sensitive to any expression of such feelings and awareness of them by others, whilst not exaggerating the importance of this aspect of the women's lives.

14.3 Male support workers may be recruited for the team with the agreement of representatives. They will need advice and support in dealing with the implications of carrying out personal care for either woman.

14.4 Support workers and families/representatives will agree to raise and discuss any concerns they have about issues of sexuality concerning the women.

14.5 All those caring for the women will agree to note any possible sexual attraction and discuss the development of any other caring relationship they observe to be developing, share observations and clarify issues.

15.0 Unforeseen problems

If not covered in either Care or House Books, advice should be sought in the first instance from the manager of the care agency. The manager will consult parents/representatives and act accordingly.

APPENDIX B.1: ISLINGTON SOCIAL SERVICES: DEPARTMENT POLICY STATEMENT PEOPLE WITH LEARNING DIFFICULTIES

1. Services are provided for people with learning difficulties by the Social Services Department as part of its responsibilities under various Acts of Parliament (National Assistance Act, Mental Health Act, CSDPA, Disabled Persons Act). Under Section 71 of the 1976 Race Relations Act there is a responsibility to meet the needs of all ethnic groups. The Departmental Race Action Plan will be used to this end.

2. United Nations resolution 3447 states, 'Disabled people have the same fundamental rights as their fellow citizens of the same age'. First and foremost people have a right to self determination and to be valued as individuals. (Guardianship under the 1983 Mental Health Act should be considered only as a positive and appropriate option using the Joint Guidelines for Staff.)

3. The department aims to ensure that the following 5 accomplishments are met:

    (i)   **Informed choice** defines and expresses individual identity. The aim is to enable and empower people to make informed choices and for them to take responsibility for the consequences of those decisions.

    (ii) **Dignity and respect** gives the experience of being valued among a network of people and of having valued roles.

    (iii) **Community presence** is the experience of having access to ordinary places that define community life, taking into account sexual, social and cultural needs.

    iv)   **Community participation** is the experience of being part of a growing network of personal relationships which include close friends.

    v)   **Competence** in developing skills to perform functional and meaningful activities with whatever assistance is required.

4. The starting point for service provision should be the assessed needs and expressed wishes of the individual and not just what is already available. That assessment should be taken to the Resources Panel and the person's needs met as fully as possible.

5. The role of the departmental care manager is to ensure that the needs of a person with learning difficulties are assessed, recognised and met. It is

essential that the person participates as fully as possible in the process and that multi-agency consultation takes place.

6. The Department has a commitment to self advocacy and recognises the role of citizen advocates for people with learning difficulties. The views of the advocate should be listened to and acted upon. For people who are unable to communicate in a way that can be easily understood this is especially important.

7. Some people behave in a way that may deny them access to community facilities and services. The challenge is in finding strategies and resources to enable that person to have that access.

8. Some people have additional needs (with resource implications), to do with mobility, vision, hearing, motivation, mental health etc., that must be taken into account at assessment.

9. People have the right to live in the community, with independence and assistance in a chosen environment. This should involve ordinary housing with single bedrooms. Admission to Mental Handicap hospital should only take place for purposes of specialist treatment and not for long stay residence. Out of Borough resources should only be used when there is no way of meeting the person's needs and expressed wishes by using or developing local resources.

10. Risk taking is an integral part of learning. Benefits, long term gain, and possible harm must be considered and reviewed before and after risk is taken.

11. If a service is not meeting a person's needs, (residential, day care or other) then it is the care manager's duty to press for improved and appropriate service provision. If a person is excluded from a service, a plan for either adapting the service to that person's needs or for finding alternative service provision must be presented by the care manager to the Resources Panel.

12. High quality co-ordination across statutory and voluntary sectors is essential in planning, policy and operational work. Agreed goal setting and maximising of resources are vital in response to the Caring for People White Paper.

13. Discriminatory practices should be identified and replaced by an awareness and sensitivity towards the particular difficulties experienced by people from minority ethnic groups. Peoples' racial and cultural characteristics should be embraced. Staffing in services should reflect the Borough's multi-racial composition.

14. People must be able to exercise their human right to be sexual within legal boundaries. Developing relationships, exploring one's sexuality, and sexual decision making are skills that must be given due consideration in assessment, training and service provision.

15. People with learning difficulties should have the same opportunities as other people to valued, rewarding and unsegregated employment and should be offered employment that is available to the rest of the community. People have the right to choose work experience and sheltered employment options.

16. Families and friends are of great importance. For people with learning difficulties it is most often the family and friends who undertake the greatest share of caring and assistance.

17. The views of the person with a learning difficulty will not always coincide with family views. Whilst attempting to reconcile these differences the Department must be clear that its obligation to the person with a learning difficulty is paramount.

APPENDIX B.2: ISLINGTON NEIGHBOURHOOD SERVICES DEPARTMENT: SERVICE AGREEMENT

SIROCKIN/WILLSON PROJECT

1. Victoria Willson and Kathy Sirockin are two Islington women with severe learning and physical disabilities previously living in residential care homes.

2. In conjunction with the women's parents, Islington Neighbourhood Services Department has developed a care package to enable the women to live in their own home together.

3. Kathy and Victoria will live in a Housing Department property on the Priory Green Estate as joint tenants.

4. Special equipment and adaptations to the property will be subject to the same criteria and regulations as for other people with disabilities living in the community.

5. Care support will be provided by (name of care agency). Additional support will come from Highbury ATC where KS currently has a 4-day-a-week place. VW will be referred to the proposed Flexi-Care Team for day care.

6. Financial arrangements:

Cost of care agency package per annum	£97,580
less ILF income per annum	£41,600
Net cost per annum £55,980	

NSD will make available to the care agency £55,980 per annum at November 1990 prices as its contribution to the cost of the care package. The existing invoice and payment mechanism in use for the care agency will be used. Apart from the standard allowance for inflation, and any change in payment rates that might be agreed by NSD covering all similar workers, no additional costs will be incurred.

7. The NSD will not be able to incur any additional costs. Arrangements will be made with the care agency for care provision within these financial limits, in consultation with the women's families.

8. If the project is not proving viable, the responsibility for the care needs of the two women will remain that of the NSD. This cannot be guaranteed to be within the proposed housing property and might be in residential units. However, the NSD is committed to the principle of ordinary housing for people with learning difficulties and would endeavour to help the clients remain living in the community.

9. If (name of care agency) are unable to continue providing care support then the NSD will consider alternative care agency provision within existing financial restraints.

10. If one of the clients moves from the property, then the care needs of the remaining individual will be reassessed with the intention of maintaining support in ordinary housing.

11. The SSD will provide named social workers for both clients. The role of the social workers will be that of care manager for respective clients pending any Departmental reorganisation in line with the requirements of the NHS and Community Care Act, 1990.

12. An operational policy has been jointly developed by parents, the care agency and social workers, within the parameters described above.

13. Reviews of the operational policy by the authors will adapt its content in line with experience gleaned from the operation of the project.

Agreed by the following parties:

(1) For Neighbourhood Services Department

. . . .

(2) For (name of care agency)

. . . .

(3) For Ms Willson

. . . .

(4) For Ms Sirockin

. . . .

APPENDIX B.8: VICTORIA'S DAILY TASKS

1. Help in getting up, bathing/showering, cleaning teeth, washing, getting ready for the day.

2. Maintaining communication through eye contact, talking to her through care and other activities, listening and responding to her facial and verbal communication.

3. Toileting and/or regular pad changes, cleaning, creaming etc.

4. Preparation of meals, snacks and drinks to her taste and needs. Support workers will normally eat with tenants.

5. At least one daily outing.

6. Daily health check e.g. colds, temperature, cuts, bruises, marks, rashes, and communication of any concerns at handover and to the care agency office and parents or representatives if appropriate.

7. Use of appropriate equipment and appliances eg. braces, splints.

8. Read diary when coming on duty.

9. Write diary entries, to include daily:

   (i) record bowel movements

   (ii) record any vomiting

   (iii) record all fit activity and take appropriate action if necessary

   (iv) record fluid intake

   (v) record any changes in normal food intake eg. loss of appetite

   (vi) record exercises completed.

10. Read House Diary when coming on duty.

11. Write in House Diary if appropriate.

12. Check for appointments, special arrangements, etc. and make any necessary arrangements, communicating with those involved, and making written notes in personal diaries or the House Diary where appropriate.

13. Arrange transport as necessary.

14. Check contents of wheelchair bag according to individual check list. Ensure that the bag is on the back of the wheelchair. Ensure suitable bicycle pump is available.

15. Sluicing, washing, drying, ironing, putting away clothes and linen.

16. Involving her in daily tasks eg. watching food preparation and cooking, laundry being put away, dusting and vacuuming, etc.

17. Playing and other sociable activities with her, including activities with her own personal items.

18. Physiotherapy maintenance routines and recording exercises.

19. Play appropriate music to her tastes.

20. Check contents of fridge and cupboards. Shop as needed, women to accompany when possible.

21. Social outings – walks, pubs, clubs, parks, visiting friends, events, etc.

22. Handover.

23. Administering medication as prescribed by doctors.

24. Social contacts, development of relationships with carers and others.

WEEKLY TASKS

1. Check stocks of medication, creams etc. and arrange for more to be ordered or bought if necessary.

2. Check supplies of incontinence pads, nappies etc. and arrange for more to be ordered if necessary.

3. Check if and when visiting parents' home.

4. Check finger and toe nails for cutting.

5. Clean combs, splints, check and clean wheelchair and wheelchair bag.

6. Check wheelchair cover and change if necessary.

7. Check wheelchair tyres, pump up if necessary. Arrange repairs if necessary. Arrange appointment at Appliance Centre if necessary. Check matrix to see if any parts are loose.

8. Draw benefits.

9. Pay bills, etc.

10. Check for appointments and arrange transport if necessary.

11. Gardening tasks as necessary.

12. Writing reports etc. as necessary, eg. for review.

13. Plan ahead for outings.

14. Housework – complete routine household cleaning and tidying.

15. Clean shoes.

16. Check on any forthcoming social arrangements eg. clubs, visits, and note and confirm any necessary arrangements.

17. Plan ahead for transport needs.

18. Check and tidy all cupboards, and shop for replacing household items in addition to food shopping.

19. Fridays – water plants indoors and outdoors.

MONTHLY TASKS

1. Check repeat prescriptions ordered and check exemption certificate valid.

2. Order incontinence supplies.

3. Check if physiotherapist should visit.

4. Check if occupational therapist should visit.

5. Check for appointments and arrange transport if necessary.

6. Check clothes and see to minor repairs; arrange replacements; sew name tags on all new clothes.

7. Check if new wheelchair cover needs to be ordered.

8. Check that adequate creams and oil supplies are in stock.

9. Check all splints, braces and boots to see if replacements are needed.

10. Check if repairs are needed – aids, equipment, household, including wheelchairs.

11. Check toys, books, equipment to see if cleaning and repairs are needed.

12. Writing reports as necessary eg. for reviews.

13. Gardening tasks as necessary.

14. Check curtains, carpets, furniture to see if cleaning is required.

15. Check all bedding and see if repair/replacement is needed.

16. On the 1st of each month – put the cleaning tape through all tape players.

17. Check validity of London Taxi cards, membership of Dial-a-Ride.

ANNUAL TASKS

Workers will facilitate holiday arrangements, spring cleaning, interior decorating, according to procedures outlined in the House Book.

APPENDIX B.9: EMERGENCIES

1. Continuous Fitting – administer rectal valium as follows:

   VICTORIA – 5 mg. of rectal valium after 3 consecutive fits. If fits continue, a further 10 mg. may be given. If fits continue, call ambulance. KATHY – as above, to a maximum of 20 mg.

2. Accidents causing physical damage eg. cuts, bruises, call an ambulance or arrange for GP visit as appropriate.

3. If either woman sleeps for 24 hours, coughs for 24 hours, listless for 24 hours, distressed for several hours, vomiting repeatedly, high temperature – call the GP for advice and a visit.

4. Pain relief – if Victoria is in pain eg. a heavy cold, period pain, headache, fever, give 2 soluble paracetomol as necessary.

5. Arrange wheelchair repairs if necessary.

Personal Finances and Welfare Benefits

N.B. Since 1991 when the project began, the names of some benefits have changed; in some cases the structure of the benefit is different and the entitlement has changed. Where applicable, the old names have been given with the new names in brackets.

BENEFITS PREVIOUSLY CLAIMED IN RESIDENTIAL ACCOMMODATION

> Severe Disablement Allowance.
>
> Income Support top up.
>
> Mobility Allowance (now Disability Living Allowance, mobility component, higher rate).
>
> Attendance Allowance (now DLA care component, highest rate). This allowance was only claimed when staying at home with parents.
>
> Community Charge exemption, in residential accommodation.

While Kathy and Victoria were in residential accommodation, the SDA and Income Support top up were largely taken as a contribution to fees, leaving a small residual 'pocket money' element for personal expenses. The women had no domestic expenses – food, lighting and heating. There was a small local authority allowance for clothing, bedding and other personal items but the parents mainly paid for these things.

BENEFITS CLAIMED IN THE INDEPENDENT LIVING SITUATION

> Severe Disability Allowance.
>
> Income Support top up.
>
> Severe Disability Premium.
>
> Mobility Allowance (now DLA mobility component, higher rate).
>
> Attendance Allowance (now DLA care component, highest rate).
>
> Housing Benefit.
>
> Community Charge/Council Tax benefit.
>
> The significant additions to income were:

1. Severe Disability Premium – an addition for living expenses.

2. Housing Benefit – this paid the full rent.

3. Attendance Allowance (DLA Care Component) was now payable full time.

However, not all of this additional income would be available for living expenses. The Independent Living Fund had agreed to finance part of the care costs. (See Chapter 4.) But the ILF informed the parents that when they calculated their contribution to care costs, the Severe Disability Premium and half the amount of the Attendance Allowance were to be taken into account as a contribution to care costs, effectively reducing the disposable income for living expenses.

With SDA, Income Support and half of the amount of the Attendance Allowance, the two women were now responsible for the following expenses:

- Food,
- Clothes,
- Toiletries, Household goods, cleaning materials, etc.,
- Bills – gas, electricity, telephone, water,
- Outings and holidays,
- Cards and presents,
- Repairs and replacements of linen, appliances, etc.
- Home decoration,
- Garden equipment and plants,
- House contents insurance.

The parents worked out that they could manage, but it was a tight budget. It was a chilling realisation of the link between disability and poverty; without continued parental subsidies their standard of living could fall dramatically.

SETTING UP HOME

The social workers applied for Social Fund Community Care grants for setting up home. Kathy was allocated £330, Victoria £700. The difference was because Victoria was allocated the funds for equipping the room for the worker sleeping in.

They needed:

- A bed each,
- A bed for the sleep-in worker,
- Dining table and chairs,
- Seating,
- Chests of drawers,
- Rugs, carpets,
- Blinds, curtains,

- Washing machine,
- Tumble Drier,
- Cooker,
- Kitchen equipment,
- Crockery and cutlery,
- Music centre,
- Bedding,
- Pictures, plants, etc.
- Hooks, towel rails, curtain fittings, etc.

The Social Fund grants paid for a new washing machine and tumble drier, essential as both women were doubly incontinent.

A second hand cooker was donated. Relatives and friends gave second hand dining table and chairs, seating, rugs, carpets, curtains, bedding, chests of drawers, a music centre.

Kathy and Victoria paid for new purpose-built beds for themselves from their small savings.

Donations from MENCAP City Foundation and some local businesses funded the furniture for the sleep-in room and new blinds for the large windows. North London Spastics Society paid for a special sofa/day bed for the lounge. House warming gifts provided extra touches such as pictures and plants.

Goods and money from all sources came to the value of about £10,000. Anyone setting up home without back up from family, friends and voluntary organisations would start off in very basic surroundings if relying on official help.

Obtaining the various benefits was not a straightforward matter. There were many delays and mistakes by the DSS. At one point Victoria's mother was told she had 'fallen off the computer' for one benefit. It took six months for it to be reinstated and in the meantime her family had to subsidise her to the amount of £2,000. Such inefficiency would have catastrophic consequences for the finances of anyone without such parental back-up.

It was clear that the meagre savings of the two women were not likely to grow very much with the level of household expenses. Where would the money come from for the re-decoration and replacement of worn items in the future? To be truly independent, the project must be self-financing; but to function above the most basic level it still needs considerable personal and financial input from families friends and voluntary organisations for things like re-decoration and replacement of worn items.

TRANSPORT COSTS

Originally it was intended that the two women would use their Mobility Allowance to fund travel, using concessionary taxi schemes and Dial-a-Ride. Their parents provided transport for hospital appointments and some other events.

These transport arrangements did not prove to be satisfactory. Booking ahead proved difficult for Dial-a-Ride. Taxis were not always reliable. Sometimes appointments were missed because one failed to turn up, or the women and their support workers were left stranded after visiting a theatre, club or concert.

In 1993 a van was purchased second-hand, with a ramp for loading wheelchair occupants. Now the women had their own transport, funded from their Mobility Allowances. The great benefit has been more independence and flexibility. The problems still to be resolved are:

1. Financing of major repairs and eventual replacement.

2. Drivers – all support workers are required to be able to drive and have a clean licence. They must be aged 25 or over to drive the van.

3. A vehicle used by several different people is not taken care of as carefully as by one user. It is not always left clean and tidy; minor problems are not reported leading to more expensive repairs; care with parking to avoid damage to the body and tyres is not always exercised.

Basic repairs are done by Lisa's father, which is convenient and beneficial, but again it represents an input which if quantified in financial terms would be considerable.

MANAGING THE MONEY

1. Household expenses

A regular sum was agreed for each woman to put into the household expenses for the week. Parents met on Sunday evenings and put this amount in a tin. Support workers were asked to keep a simple account book to note all purchases. The amount was increased as necessary.

2. Personal expenses

A similar system was operated for personal expenses. Each woman had a tin into which an agreed weekly amount was placed. Purchases were noted in a simple account book.

3. Household bills

A joint account for bills was set up for the two women. They paid an agreed amount in on a regular basis. Cheques were drawn on this account to pay household bills.

4. Collecting benefits

Benefits are still collected by parents as appointees, and paid into personal accounts held for this purpose by each of the two women. Eventually parents would like staff to assume this appointee role. However, further discussions will be necessary as it is not simply a matter of drawing the money, but of managing it on behalf of the two women.

5. Accounting

Accounting for money spent must be done so that there can be no cause for suspicion about how it has been spent. Even simple accounts are not always kept consistently. At some point the question of money management must be addressed as otherwise the project will never run independently of the parents.

APPLYING FOR BENEFITS

Anyone doing this on behalf of someone with profound intellectual and multiple disabilities should not underestimate the time and frustration which will be involved. Victoria's and Kathy's situations were complicated by moving from residential accommodation, where one set of benefits was applicable to independent living, where different rules applied; by moving address; and in Kathy's case by moving from one borough and DSS office to another.

Despite input by social workers and the borough's welfare rights officer, and persistence by parents, obtaining all these benefits was a long drawn out process.

Some points to note if you are doing this:

1. Take a photocopy of all benefit application forms before completing them. Complete the copy in rough to keep, and then copy the details on to the original.

2. Get a certificate of posting to establish the date and proof of application.

3. Date and keep a copy of any letter you write in connection with applications.

4. Use an up to date copy of one of the basic references such as the Disability Rights Handbook to check entitlement, methods of application and appeals. (Available from The Disability Alliance Educational and Research Association, Universal House, 88–94 Wentworth Street, London E1 7SA. Tel: 071–247 8776.)

6. Severe Disability Premium (an add-on to Income Support) can only be claimed on behalf of someone suffering the prescribed degree of disability AND living independently ie. no one can be claiming Invalid Care Allowance for looking after them. Kathy and Victoria satisfied these conditions. Their care was provided by professionals; no one received ICA for looking after them. They were tenants in their own home; it was not shared with relatives; and neither was dependent on the other.

7. Most people with profound intellectual and multiple disabilities receive SDA with Income Support top-up. Although this amounts to no more than the alternative entitlement to Income Support, SDA should always be claimed as it is non-means tested and not subject to any limit on savings.

If such a project is to be financially viable, all entitlements to benefit must be investigated and pursued. Anyone managing money on behalf of someone like

Kathy or Victoria must budget meticulously, and also keep a note of any savings to make sure these do not take them out of entitlement to some benefits.

There are many other issues when managing finances in this situation – medium term planning for clothes, holidays, etc; managing any money which may be left or given to them; keeping up to date with changes in benefits and government regulations.

(There is more detailed information about benefits and managing money on behalf of people with profound intellectual and multiple disabilities in *Listen to Me*, Pat Fitton, Jessica Kingsley Publishers, 1994, especially Chapter 15, Benefits and Chapter 22, The Future.)

The Household Budget

VICTORIA'S PERSONAL EXPENDITURE

	Weekly	*Per Year*
Income		
Income support & Severe Disablement Allowance	£86.95	£4,521.40
Mobility Allowance (component of Disability Living Allowance)	£31.00	£1,612.00
Attendance Allowance (Care Component of DLA – half of total; see Appendix C)	£22.85	£1,188.20
	£140.80	£7,321.60
Expenditure		
Gas	£8.50	£442.00
Electricity	£6.50	£338.00
Telephone	£5.00	£260.00
Water	£2.50	£130.00
Insurance	£3.70	£192.40
Vehicle and other transport	£20.00	£1,040.00
Clothes	£5.00	£260.00
Replacements & repairs	£5.00	£260.00
Food & cleaning materials	£25.00	£1,300.00
Personal – Outings, tapes, toiletries	£25.00	£1,300.00
		£5,522.40
Reserves		
Holidays, vehicle contingencies and savings	£34.60	£1799.20
	£140.80	£7,321.60

Notes:

1. Severe Disability Premium (£32.55) is taken for care costs in accordance with ILF rules.

2. Families subsidise:
   - household equipment
   - clothing
   - re-decorating
   - vehicle servicing and repairs

labour – garden, household repairs

3. Charitable grants needed.
4. Gifts.

HOUSEHOLD BUDGET FOR THE YEAR FOR LISA AND VICTORIA

Services

Gas	884.00	
Electricity	676.00	
Telephone	520.00	
Water Rates	260.00	
	£2,340.00	£2,340.00

Insurance

House Insurance		
Washing/Drier Insurance	£384.80	£384.80

Vehicle

Tax	120.00	
M.O.T.	26.00	
A.A.	31.00	
Insurance	471.00	
Petrol	800.00	
Repairs	600.00	
Other transport, taxis etc.	32.00	
	£2,080.00	£2,080.00

Personal

Food and cleaning materials	2,600.00	
Personal-toiletries, outings including workers expenses	2,600.00	
Clothes	£520.00	£5720.00

Replacing Household Equipment

Including redecoration, new furniture and furnishings, appliances, cleaning carpets etc.	£1040.00	£1040.00

Reserves

For vehicle, holidays, other eventualities and emergencies	£3,078.40	£3,078.40
		£14,643.20

Tell Them About Me – The Care Book

As Pat Fitton explains in her book *Listen to Me* I too found I had to tell many different people about Victoria, in a variety of situations, as she had to with her daughter Kathy. Victoria cannot tell people herself how she feels, what she enjoys doing and what she needs to keep her happy and comfortable. If she has a pain it is not always easy to work out exactly where it is, or what may be making her uncomfortable. She has a wide range of shouts, cries and sounds, and unless you know her well you cannot always work out whether she is really very upset due to pain or discomfort, whether she is just bored, or whether she would like something to eat or drink, or wants to go out. Victoria grabs at anything interesting – objects, furniture, people – and can push things aside quite powerfully. She has no idea of the consequences of these actions and does not realise that she can cause serious damage and sometimes hurt people.

I found it was vital to give everyone who might come across Victoria information quickly, clearly and preferably, graphically. This originated from the short periods of time when she had to go into hospital. Nurses needed to know that Victoria could not talk or recognise danger. She might throw things such as bowls of water oxygen cylinders very quickly, and would eat small objects such as thermometers. I made up a series of cards covered in plastic with essential information so that when I was not on the ward, everyone would know how Victoria would react. As time went by, I gradually included things like her personality, how she tried to communicate, what she enjoyed doing, as well as details about her daily care needs and medical requirements.

These cards proved very valuable at school and when she went on the Kith & Kids 2 to 1 Projects (See pages 14 and 14a of her Care Book)

When Victoria and Kathy came to live together, Pat and I found we had used similar methods, and it was at this stage that I adopted the Care Book style. I took the same headings as Kathy's, so that it would be simpler for support workers to use. I used a A4 plastic covered booklet with transparent plastic sleeves which is durable, can travel, and enables individual items to be updated.

We have tried to ensure that her Care Book reflects what Victoria wants and needs. When we update it we include not just changes in medication and her medical conditions, but new skills and interests she has developed.

This is how Victoria's care book was put together – the pages shown are mainly those explaining and illustrating Victoria and her care.

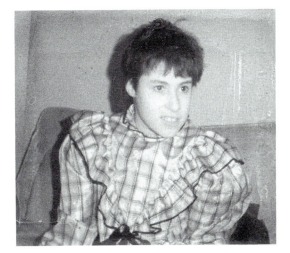

Victoria's Care Book

CONTENTS

This makes it easy for carers to look up a topic quickly. It also gives an idea of the wide range of needs of the person you care for.

Victoria Willson: Her Book

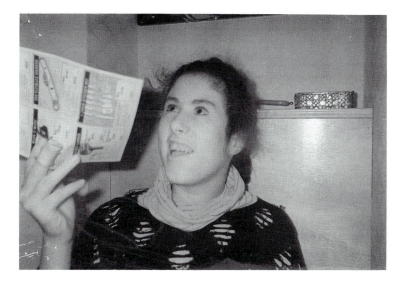

The purpose of this book is:

* To give you some basic information about Victoria

* To give guidance on Victoria's basic care routines

This explains what the book is for, and shows a photograph of Victoria in her parent's house, relaxed and happy, to show carers how she can be at her best.

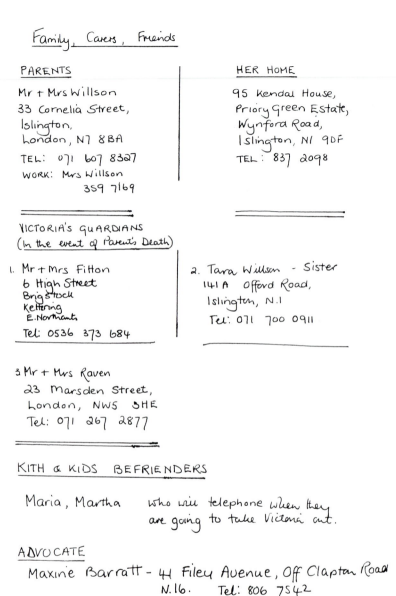

Family, Carers, Friends

PARENTS

Mr + Mrs Willson
33 Cornelia Street,
Islington,
London, N7 8BA
TEL: 071 607 8327
WORK: Mrs Willson
                359 7169

HER HOME

95 Kendal House,
Priory Green Estate,
Wynford Road,
Islington, N1 9DF
TEL: 837 2098

VICTORIA'S GUARDIANS
(In the event of Parents' Death)

1. Mr + Mrs Fitton
   6 High Street
   Brigstock
   Kettering
   E. Northants
   Tel: 0536 373 684

2. Tara Willson - Sister
   141 A Offord Road,
   Islington, N.1
   Tel: 071 700 0911

3 Mr + Mrs Raven
  23 Marsden Street,
  London, NW5 3HE
  Tel: 071 267 2877

KITH & KIDS BEFRIENDERS

Maria, Martha   who will telephone when they
                 are going to take Victoria out.

ADVOCATE

Maxine Barratt - 44 Filey Avenue, Off Clapton Road
                N.16.   Tel: 806 7542

These pages give the essential contact details for Victoria's family, and close friends who would supervise her care if we both died. The names of the GP, hospital and consultants have been changed. This information ensures that in an emergency carers are able to contact those close to Victoria and those who can give medical advice if needed. Often problems can be resolved by a talk over the telephone. If Victoria is taken ill or has an accident, we would want to join her as quickly as possible in hospital or wherever she might be.

<u>Victoria Willson</u>:   <u>Date of Birth</u>   <u>26 June 1970</u>

Nat. Ins. No.   ** ** ** **
Dial-A-Ride: ** ***   Tel:
Attendance Allow: ** ***
Mobility   *** *x* ***

<u>Doctors</u>   <u>Telephone</u>

Dr. W. White   Appointments   1071 —
Group Practice   General Enquiries
Brown Road   EMERGENCY

<u>Hospitals</u>   _____

<u>Dr. P. Pink</u>   X Hospital   1071 —
(for TS and   London
general health)

Hosp. No. 1234

<u>Dr. G. Green</u>   Orthopedic Hospital   1071 —
                         London
- for scoliosis

- for brace,   B. Orthopedic Hospital   1081 —
  splints and boots   Middx.

		Telephone
Distict Nurses	Windsor Health Clinic Station Road	
	9 - 4 pm	1071 —
	After Hours	1071 —
Dentist	Mooreway Health Centre Brick Lane	1071 —
Physiotherapy	Community Team for People with Learning Disabilities Dawson Street	1071 —
Occupational Therapists	Mooreway Health Centre Brick Lane	1071 —
Continence Advisor	Central Clinic Main Street	1071 —
Continence Supplies	Supplies Office Station Road	1071 —
Social Worker	Ray Robin Neighboorhood Office Downs Avenue	1071 —

Victoria's Condition

Victoria had Tuberous Sclerosis from birth. This has affected the development of her brain, so she has severe learning and physical disabilities; and her skin with white skin patches on trunk, arms and legs.

From the age of 6 weeks, she has had convulsions, ranging from slight tremours to salaam spasms to tonic clonic fits.

At 9 months she had a series of convulsions and went into a status coma for 3 months. When she came out her left side was paralized.

At age eight, she developed ⟶ scoliosis of the spine, and has had to wear a body brace for 23 hours

At ages 9/10 she had operations on her feet to release the tendons so she could stand. Aged 12 she learnt to walk, with assistance, but splints were necessary because of her weak legs, mobile ankles and delicate feet.

At age 10 she developed Adenoma Sebaceum = rash of red spots over the nose.

This explains very briefly Victoria's various disabilities and medical conditions. It gives information in date order, so that readers can see how some of her difficulties have increased over the years.

Victoria's Drugs and Medical Requirements

She must be given the following daily :-

9 am.	Epilim tablets	100mgs × 4	= 420 mgs
	Tegratol tablets	100 mgs × 1 200 mgs × 1	= 300 mgs
3 pm.	Epilim tablets	100 mgs × 4	= 400 mgs.
9 pm.	Epilim tablets	500 mgs × 1 100 mgs × 3	= 800 mgs
	Tegratol tablets	100 mgs × 1 200 mgs × 1	= 300 mgs.

Emergency

VALIUM   5 mg rectal tubes   Found in Fridge
(Stesolid Diazapam)

To be used when she has had 3 consecutive fits

SKIN

IMPORTANT Do not use ANY perfumed
items on her skin at anytime

SPRILON SPRAY   Use on her body to prevent rubbing by brace.
BALNEUM BATH OIL   Use daily in bath, helps excema + dryness
BETNOVATE   Hydro cortizone cream when excema is bad.
VASELINE   For face and hands for dryness
MOISTURE CREAMS   For face and body

To re order any of the above, see instructions in House Book.

These explain the purpose of Victoria's various anti-convulsants. They refer to the House Book for instructions on re-ordering prescribed medicines, creams and oils. They also explains how to give the medication, where it is kept, and why it is important to give it at exact times.

How to give Victoria pills

Victoria must always have her medication as these prevent her from having fits. They need to be given at EXACTLY those times stated to give her maximum even coverage of medication throughout the 24 hours.

All medication is kept in the small cupboard next to the shower room in Victoria's bedroom, 2nd shelf down. They are in a white plastic box and instructions are on yellow in plastic folder.

Victoria will chew the pills quite nicely, but they have a horrid taste, so if given by themselves will give her a very unpleasant taste in her mouth for hours afterwards so :–

1. Count out millegrams to number of pills

2. Prepare a drink, or food to give afterwards.

3. Gather all pills together and push <u>all</u> of them into her mouth at once, telling her beforehand that you are going to give her her pills.

4. Gently holding her right hand, offer food or drink.

5. After <u>every</u> meal clean her teeth thoroughly as this helps get rid of taste and removes food.

6. Record pills given in Victoria's diary by ticking medication box giving <u>exact</u> time.

What sort of person is Victoria?

Victoria is a positive person, and knows who and what she likes.
She is very responsive to physical contact, talk and play.

She can get very upset, very quickly

This could be one, or all of the following: -

1. Discomfort
   Wants to lay down
   sit up
   walk
   wet/soiled
2. Hunger - Victoria has a good appetite!

3. Boredom - please do something different

4. Epileptic Activity - Sleepiness, need to lay down, general unpleasant feelings, possibly headache, fretfulness, screams.

The idea of this page is to establish Victoria as an individual in her own right, not just someone with a lot of problems. This page shows two pictures of Victoria, one very cheerful and relaxed, the other when she was unhappy. Her personality is described and her sometimes rapid mood changes are explained.

Victoria Likes

* Playing with paper, especially noisy shiny stuff

* Listening to music, classical, good tunes, jazz, Flying Pickets - mozart

* Laying on the floor with 'bits' a music

* Sitting in her chairs watching activity - with a group at home, visiting friends, in the pub, in a resturant.

* Cuddles, someone talking to her.

* Flicking plastic bottles that make a noise

The next two pages describe and illustrate Victoria's favoured activities. The photographs help others to see that she has a wide range of interests and enjoys going out to many different places.

<u>Victoria also likes</u>

* Going for walks
* Travelling in vehicles
* Shopping
* City life - traffic & bustle!

* Going out with
  Martha + Maria

* Swimming

  that is
  splashing
  and drinking
  the pool!

Communication

Victoria communicates through facial expressions, and through a series of different sounds with which she is able to express her needs.

Aged 14

* "Eeeeh" + smile =

  Hello, I'm happy enjoying this!

* She will watch others; smile with approval; quite good eye contact

* A sharp shout usually means "Come and take me of toilet or get me out of bed."

* "Aaah" low moan, means more food, I've got nothing to touch, plse look at me

* Aaah louder + frown means I'm definately NOT HAPPY, I do not like this, I'm wet, fed up LOOK AT ME NOW - HELP!

It is important that Victoria is talked through every activity of the day, so that she has the opportunity to learn to understand simple language & commands.

Aged 9

These pages explain how Victoria communicates her needs and wishes, as she does not talk.

1993 - Victoria now 'eye points to things she chooses
So, if she looks at a piece of toast, looks at you - she is
telling you she wants the toast! This should be built
on, so watch carefully and let her choose the items. Always
ask her what she wants, and repeat the object chosen.

Facilitation Communication

Anne Emmerson a speech Therapist is visiting
Victoria to teach everyone who works with Victoria + Lisa
this revolutionary new method of communication.

After you have been shown the method of making
Victoria 'POINT TO OBJECTS' it is essential everyone
follows the same proceedure.

We will concentrate on the following 6 items that
are really important to Victoria. Show her the real
things, get her to point, and give them to her
immediately.

FOOD — show and name the food

CUP — show her the cup, name the drink

MUSIC — get her to touch the unit where
the stereo is, and turn on music

BED — show her the bed, lay her down

FLOOR — "Lay down?" Point to floor,
lay her down.

GO OUT — Point to front door. Go out

SHOUTING

If Victoria shouts, she is, we think trying very hard to
tell you what she wants. We suggest you offer her
the 6 items first. You're on your own after that!

Victoria Feeds Herself

She uses a spoon or fingers, as appropriate.

She can pick up a cup to give herself a drink.

Try to sit on her left, so that you can see how much food is going in her mouth, and not on the floor! If you lift the apron, this minimises loss of food.

These pages show pictures of Victoria eating and drinking. There is an explanation of how she gives herself food and drink, what she enjoys and what she dislikes. Suggestions are given for dealing with situations when she is having problems with eating.

Meal Times

* Prepare food, and allow to cool down, Victoria does not like hot food. Have everything to hand.

* offer her a spoonful, if she accepts it give her the spoon to feed herself.

* After the first frantic rapid eating, talk to her and encourage her to slow down "gently" This can be done by softly placing your hand on top of her right hand.

* Offer a glass of water half way through meal.

* If she throws the spoon, hold her hand, offer a drink.

* If she continues to throw spoon, food and plate remove the plate - she is probably not hungry.

* If she finishes the meals offered, and continues to moan, she is probably still hungry. Offer more food, encourage fruit eating.

* She can be 'upset' at mealtimes, often this is because we are not reading her "body signs" Keep calm, talk her through alternatives; check to see if wet; if all else fails take her away from the table. If you think she is still hungry offer refused food later.

Bon appetite !

VICTORIA'S EPILEPTIC SEIZURES

We believe Victoria is having Complex Partial Seizures and the type and frequency has recently changed, and you should note the following facts.

These seizures happen when her ordinary brain activity is suddenly disrupted.

Seizures can taken many forms, since the brain is responsible for such a wide range of functions. Intelligence, personality, mood, memory, sensations, movement and consciousness are all controlled within the brain; any of these functions may be temporarily disturbed during the course of an epileptic seizure.

Victoria has the following:-

Generalized Seizures

Are: Gasping breath
            Arms above her head, turning inwards
            Legs stiffen
            Arms and legs jerk quite sharply
            Eyes race or move from left to right
            If standing she will crash over
            Last 10 - 15 seconds

Recovery   She usually comes round quickly, smiles and carries
            on

When the happen   Dropping off to sleep
                  During the night
                  On waking
                  But they can happen during the day at any time

Absences

Are brief interruption of consciousness and in Victoria she stares, her pupils are quite still, or her eyelids flutter,and she may dribble.
These can happen any time.

Partial Seizures

Involves part of her brain responsible for mood and emotion.

Are: Sensory disturbance - we suspect something that is
            happening within her body which is frightening her
            Look of fear, eyes starting, generally very upset
            Lips quiver and tears flow
            Plucking or picking of her clothes or skin
            Pushing things or people away from her voilently
            Thrashing about, stomping her legs

These pages summarise the main types of fit Victoria experiences.
They give carers details of action required. There is a reminder that every fit must be recorded in her fit chart, which is kept at the front of her diary. A consistent system of recording all fit activity must be carried out by all who care for someone with epilepsy, so that any patterns may emerge. Frequency, type and length must all be carefully noted. These charts can then be used by doctors for diagnostic purposes.

Happen: Any time
            But she can sometimes be diverted by talking or
            changing her situation eg move her to another room

What to do: Ideally, remove her splints and boots and lay her
            on her bed, or on the floor.
            Comfort her if you can
            Once 'terror' is over, wash her face and hands
            Let her rest/sleep if she wants to.

Complex Partial Seizures

Again involves part of her brain responsible for mood and
emotions.

Are: Breathing may stop, or is very laboured
            She will stiffen, with arms straight above her head
            Her pupils will roll up under her eyelids
            Last 10 - 30 seconds

What to do: DO NOT attempt to restrain her movements
            Her breathing will resume to normal
            Make sure she is laying down with something under
            head for a pillow
            After the seizure, roll her onto her side
            (recovery position).

She may feel muddled and confused, and will need reassurance.
She might want to sleep, or get up and continue with what she
she was doing.

MORE THAN ONE SEIZURE

If one seizure follows another, or she is not awake after
½ hour, or there is troubling breathing - medical help must be
summoned.

What to do;   3 Seizures- with deep sleep in between
              Gently wash her face, gently brush her hair
              Get her sitting in a chair or wheelchair
              Open window, or take her into some fresh air

If Seizures continue or you cannot wake her -

             PHONE   FOR ADVICE

             PARENTS WILL BE CONTACTED FOR ADVICE

If either contact are not made within 10 minutes then contact
her GP Dr.   for advice

Dial 999 if seizures continue. Inform   Take
medication with you.

IT IS VERY IMPORTANT TO MONITOR AND CAREFULLY RECORD ALL FIT
AND SEIZURE ACTIVITY. THIS IS DONE ON DAY SHEET OF HER DIARY
AND FIT RECORD SHEET IN FRONT OF HER DIARY.

FITS

4. <u>Daytime</u> - Temporal Lobe Epilepsy

During the last 6 years Victoria has experienced stages/periods in her life where her fits change, and she presents 'unusual' behaviour due to fit activity

These periods may include any or all of the following:-
   * Increased sleepiness and lethargy
   * Unpleasant feelings
   * possibly headaches
   * dribbling saliva

She will then present the following behaviour:-
   - general unhappiness
   - fretfulness, difficult to please
   - be off her food, or picky with drinks + food
   - mood swings - voicing these by moaning
   - apathy
   - distressed & distraught - for no apparent reason become very upset, moans loudly leading up to screaming, red in face, pushing people, stamping feet, crying tears. At this stage she will use strong eye contact with you, almost asking you to stop whatever it is.

We have experienced these episodes as patterns over the years, and sometimes there are no immediate answers.
   However, it is essential to record well, and we have devised a monitoring form that is opposite the daily diary page.
   IT IS IMPORTANT to fill in unusual behaviour not only for fits, but as part of Tuberous Sclerosis condition. See page .   of this book

UNUSUAL BEHAVIOUR

Victoria has a condition whereby tumours can form in any part of her body, anytime. She can also develop hydrocephalus, because of her brains lesions.

So, if any of these show signs of devoping in Victoria:-
- Severe vomitting
- Severe diarrhoea
- looks as if she is in great pain
- deep sleep, almost unconscious
- really bizarre, prolonged behaviour.

then the following steps MUST BE TAKEN

1. Inform Jean + Norman Willson; in their absence Maxine her advocate, or Pat + Barrie Fitton.

2. Next stage — after say 2/3 weeks of distressed periods not diminishing it is essential to get Victoria checked by her G.P. This is for physical illness e.g. sore throat, urine infection etc. If all is clear, then an urgent appointment at National Hospital is necessary. Her condition, particularly the tumours and epilepsy means she must be checked by experts thoroughly. In particular her drug levels. The importance of giving the doctors a pattern of her behaviour during the previous weeks/months is crucial.
If all is well, then it usually means that a new pattern of 'fit activity' has emerged. This does not mean she has actual fits, but her behaviour is showing changes in her brain patterns, as a consequence of fit activity.

This page explains what carers should do if Victoria has any really unusual behaviour, as with her condition of Tuberous Sclerosis, this could be an indication of the development of a tumour somewhere in her body. Often carers will talk over the telephone with her parents about their concerns, and appropriate action can usually be agreed on fairly quickly.

Unusual Behaviour 6ont.
DURING THE STAGES

Victoria is very frightened and unhappy because she does not know what is going on. It is important that everyone involved with her tries to reassure her, keeps calm, and ensures she does not damage herself or others.

Try Diversion Tactics

Sometimes you can divert her by giving favourite objects e.g. the flicking paper or plastic bottles, but try these too:-

- Walk her to the bathroom or sink, turn on the taps and let her run her hand in water
- give her an ice cube in her hand
- turn the hairdryer gently on her face/hands.
- use her body massager on her body
- lay her in her bed or on floor with LOUD CALMING MUSIC eg. Enya, Mozart
- Give her Rescue Remedy on her tongue, a few drops.

If she is really ~~uncontrollable~~, and to stop her hysteria, because that is what it is :-

- Lay her down, away from furniture + people.
- Turn her on her side, cover with a blanket, to keep her arms and legs from thrashing about

- Stroke her face, giving comforting sounds "you're fine, it will soon pass etc."

- try calming music too

Sometimes there is nothing that seems to stop her, just have to leave her alone till whatever it is passes. She often tires herself out - just let her sleep. Wash her face + hands, gently brush her hair when she returns to normal.

This page explains the other unusual behaviour which is though to be related to fit activity. It shows clearly some activities that may divert Victoria, and the action that must be taken if all else fails. The main purpose of this page is to reassure carers that there are times when Victoria has to be left alone, although the carer will remain close by.

SKIN CARE

Victoria skin is very delicate round the feet area, and vigilance is required for pressure sores and it is essential boots are put on properly.

Excema: on hands and arms, use Balneum bath daily oil (on prescription) She will try to relieve itching by rubbing arm on table, carpet. It is essential to wipe off food after meals. Treat with Betnovate if open, but twice daily applying E45 will keep it under control.

FACE: Is dry, so use face moisture lotions and Vaseline at night.

BRACE: Look for pressure patches daily, apply dressing if skin breaks down. Use Sprilon spray for prevent.

SOAP: Use simple or non-perfumed variety

AFTER BATH: Use cream to moisturise - NO TALC!

HAIR: Use good shampoo, always conditioner Occasional HEnna treatment.
Usually washed not more than twice a week because of dryness. Victoria loves her hair brushed, but do not tie too tightly, as it damages + causes split ends.

NAILS: Must be trimmed weekly with nail clippers, + then emery board used. Scratching herself + others is then kept to a minimum !!

This explains why Victoria's skin is very delicate and details the action required to prevent it from breaking down.

TOILET TIME

Victoria does not like to be wet, and she is very pleased when she uses the toilet - so try these times

* on waking
* after breakfast
* mid morning
* after lunch
* mid afternoon
* after dinner

Please walk her to toilet!

She has a history of constipation, so careful thought has to go into her diet with plenty of fibre and fluids, especially water, vegetables and fruit

ON TOILET
- This may take from 5 mins onwards
- To stop hand biting - give usual paper to flick
- Respond quickly to her "I've Been" signals otherwise wailing will follow. Give PRAISE

CHANGING
- Encourage holding onto bars
- Try and wipe clean if wet, always if soiled. Use wet ones if out.
- Use vaseline around vagina, area and anus to prevent chapping

This page explains Victoria's needs arising from her double incontinence. It gives basic instructions for when she uses the toilet, changing her pads, and the reasons and procedure for cleaning and creaming after she has used the toilet or been changed.

PERIODS

Victoria has periods regularly, which last 3/4 days.

It is vital that accurate records are made, on her fit chart, first page of the diary, for the following reasons :-

> * About a week before, her moods will
> change. Sometimes, not always, she
> will be any or all of the following :-
> loud, boisterous
> miserable, listless
> aggressive, pushy

> * She sometimes has a fit (s) during this
> pre·week, and sometimes when the period
> starts.

Victoria wears her usual continence pads during her period, but extra washing and bathing are required for personal hygiene.

On the first day, she may be in pain - often a grey face, cloudy eyes with. lines around, she will be (sometimes) miserable. GIVE HER A PARACETOMOL

This page discusses Victoria's periods, how to deal with them and how to record them. It also shows how to tell if Victoria is in pain, and when to give her pain relief.

SPLINTS and BOOTS

Victoria's legs and feet are weak, and must be kept in correct position for as long as possible

SPLINTS Keep them in correct position, make sure right + left are put on corresponding feet!
Wipe clean once, twice a week with damp cloth.
Do not pull straps too hard.
Always put on long socks to prevent rubbing
Check feet daily for pressure sores, chilblains, blisters, + bruising.

BOOTS Leather boots, with splints give right support for walking.
When putting on _ make sure right toes are laying as flat as possible by holding down with your fingers.
  - Ensure <u>both</u> little flaps, under the tongue of the boot ARE FLAT - if folded over these will create blisters + PAIN!
  - Tie the laces firmly.

Clean with shoe polish twice a week.

OTHER SHOES Trainers keep for social outings only.

Slippers after bath, or if feet are damaged.
Be careful when she walks with slippers
Small socks should be put on at night because her feet get cold.

This gives instructions for fitting splints, boots and shoes correctly, to maintain the best position for Victoria's feet and legs.

WALKING and STANDING

FREE STANDING

In the toilet, Victoria can hold onto both Hold rails to have her skirt or trousers pulled down to be washed and changed.

In the kitchen she can stand at the sink to 'wash up'

To help Victoria stand up, ask her "please stand up" and prompt her left hand onto seat arm, using your right hand, grasp her right hand and gently touch her right shoulder. This should motivate her quite quickly into a standing position, and you should not have to lift her or bear any strain yourself. Unfortunately, she does not balance well yet and the feet will be anxious to be off, so you have to be pretty smart to either walk her with both your hands, or place her hands on her frame. So its essential to have the frame ready.

WALKING

Victoria loves to walk, but especially with purpose ie to the kitchen for a meal! Inside the house try to walk her everywhere. It is best to use the frame, so that she does not use your body to lean on, and takes her own balance; but for short journeys you can balance her quite nicely.
She should always be walked from house to car and visa versa When out, she loves to walk on grass or just on paths in the park, this helps to keep her circulation going in the feet and legs when it is especially cold.

SITTING

It is very important that Victoria continues to backstep to any chair, and prompt her by saying "Please step back"

CARS

Victoria knows what cars are, and takes great pride into getting into and out of cars! Use the same procedure as normal chairs, but ask her to lift her legs over, holding her left hand, with your right hand on her left shoulder ask her to "Sit Up Straight please" this she does very nicely, thus not straining YOUR body and back'

Aug 90 with Gordelle.

This page explains why it is important that Victoria stands and walks purposefully and gives guidance when and where this should happen.

BRACE

Victoria has to wear this for 12 hours, a day. So she can go to bed without it, but it must be on by 9.30 am to 9 pm = 12 HOURS (curvature of the spine) in a good position. IT IS ESSENTIAL SHE WEARS IT.

She has been wearing a brace since she was 10 years old, so is very used to it and it being taken on and off, so she will co-operate

TO PUT BRACE ON

It usually takes two people to put the brace on, but with time and confidence, one person can do it!

1. Put T shirt on first, these are kept bottom drawer of dressing table.

2. Stand Victoria up, 1st person holding her arms round their neck.

3. 2nd person wraps the brace round her body, working from the back, making sure hip curves of brace are resting on Victoria's hips.

4. 1st person then turns her round to face 2nd person.

5. 2nd person will then do up middle strap. To thread pass strap through first gap, then back through second gap, thus ensuring strap is secure. Gaps should be approx 2"

6. Then lay Victoria on bed or floor:-

    Pull T shirt down, so there are not too many creases

    for comfort, push bosoms into place between the brace holes,

    thread other two straps. NEVER FORCE STRAPS

    dress with other clothes

These pages explain that because of her scoliosis, Victoria needs to wear a body brace during the day. They give step by step instructions on fitting and removing her brace, when it should be removed and they also note how to keep it in good order.

BRACE

TO TAKE BRACE OFF

The straps are easy release, just push the white tongue in, unthread strap and peel off brace.

7 - 8 p.m. is a good time to take it off, after supper, so it can be taken off in the toilet. Victoria can then use the toilet without her brace. This sometimes is the time for a bowel movement, if she does go, please respond immediately if she yells "I' ve Been!"
It also gives her an opportunity to feel and scratch her own body. IMAGINE THE WONDERFUL FEELING THIS GIVES HER.

After the toilet, lay her lay on the floor for awhile, she loves this freedom time and will often use it to shuffle round the room.

Last part of the hour use:-

       Body Massage

       Physio excercises

BRACE MAINTENANCE

1. Wipe daily with sponge for hygiene.

2. Sponge clean the straps, especially top strap for food marks.

3. Check daily pressure marks on Victoria's body.

4. Check daily brace straps are working.

FOR BRACE REPAIRS/REPLACEMENT - Stanmore

WHEELCHAIR

Victoria has a NHS wheelchair, which folds down to go into the boot of a normal car.

It has two cushions, which should be positioned as follows: –

* Firm thin cushion is for the back

* Soft cushion is the seat and should be pushed as far back till it touches the back of the wheelchair

Victoria uses her wheelchair for most journeys <u>outside</u> the house. Inside she should walk. It should not be used at mealtimes as it usually does not fit under a table, and will get very messy. However, sometimes at social events it is the only way!

Victoria <u>must</u> be strapped in AT ALL TIMES, and the brakes must always be on, especially when she is back stepping

MAINTENANCE

The wheelchair needs a good weekly wash, with a wipe down as required.
Check belt and brakes are always correct.
If bolts, screws etc. drop out — save them.
Norman does weekly check and minor repairs.
Anything larger contact: <u>Elmsleigh Invacar</u> -Tel: 0268 792761
Please quote: <u>Victoria's Reference No. 8/50364</u>
          <u>Chair Type – Carters 8NC 25546 77 Q.</u>
                    <u>16"×17" Seat</u>
O/T or physio organises new wheelchairs

This gives a brief summary of what Victoria's wheelchair is like, with the reference number and details of where to get adjustments and repairs. There are brief details on how to keep it clean and in good repair.

VICTORIA WILLSON

EXERCISE PROGRAMME

APRIL 1993

BEFORE ASSISTING VICTORIA WITH THIS PROGRAMME CONSULT WITH A
CHARTERED PHYSIOTHERAPIST.

This programme addresses Victoria's three main physical problems.
The programme is most effective if it is incorporated into her
daily life rather than just being used in isolation.

The aims are to prevent worsening of Victoria's scoliosis (side-
ways curve of the spine), to promote her use and awareness of
her left side (particularly her arm) and to maintain and improve
her walking.

These first exercises should be carried out during the one hour
of the day when Victoria does not wear her spinal brace:

1.   Stretching Victoria's Scoliosis:
      Victoria lies on her right side with two pillows or the
      roll under the most convex part of her scoliosis. The
      helper faces Victoria at her waist level, crosses his/her
      hands, places one on her lower ribs and the other on her
      pelvis (hip bone). The helper uses this hand hold to main-
      tain Victoria's side lying position and then gently and
      smoothly pushes ribs and pelvis apart. Pressure should be
      distributed evenly through the whole hand. A full stretch
      is maintained for a count of 5 and the slowly released.
      repeat 5 times.

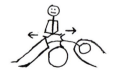

These pages make it clear that it is essential for Victoria to have regular physiotherapy in addition to as much natural and normal movement as possible. The
physiotherapist has drawn positions that should be avoided by Victoria.

2. **Prone lying:**
    This exercise gives a general stretch to Victoria's spine.
    Victoria lies on her tummy with the foam roll under her
    upper thorax with arms over it. A cushion or pillow under
    Victoria's hips will concentrate the stretch on the upper
    back rather than the lower back which is already very
    mobile.

    Victoria could carry out an activity in this position, which
    should be maintained for 10-15 minutes minimum.

3. **Left side sitting**
    This position stretches Victoria's scoliosis and promotes
    weight bearing on, and therefore more awareness of, her left
    side. Victoria may need help to achieve and maintain this
    position for 10-15 minutes. Again an activity can be
    carried out in this position.

Victoria should wear her brace, splits and boots for the rest of
this programme.

4. **Use of left arm**
    Victoria should sit as squarely as possible in her chair.
    The helper is positioned to her left and uses touch,
    attractive objects and different textures to encourage
    movement and awareness of her left arm. Short times should
    be made for this throughout the day.

5.   Standing and walking
*   NB. Victoria must wear her splits and boots when walking.
      Victoria should never need to use her wheelchair indoors but
      should always walk between rooms;   additionally Victoria can
      be encouraged to walk short distances outside (e.g. to a
      car, to the end of the estate). The type of support given
      to Victoria should be varied and include bilateral support,
      support on the right, support of the left (which Victoria
      finds most difficult) and use of the gutter frame.

      It is important that Victoria use good, safe patterns of
      movement when standing and sitting. To stand her feet
      should be flat on the floor just in front in the seat (any
      foot rests must be pushed out of the way), she should assist
      by pushing on the arms of the chair and should come forwards
      and up.

      To sit Victoria should step back until her legs touch the
      seat, she should put her hands onto the chair arms and lower
      down to sitting, bending at hips and knees.

6.   Side-stepping
      This helps Victoria to learn to control the weight
      transference necessary for balance when walking. Supporting
      Victoria from in front she is guided to step sideways.
      Ensure that side stepping takes place in both directions.

In order to facilitate use of different styles of walking a planned daily routine may be useful so that, for example, Victoria walks from bed to bathroom with bilateral support, from bedroom to kitchen with the gutter frame, from kitchen to sitting-room side stepping to the left, etc.

If you have any questions or concerns about this programme consult a chartered physiotherapist.

PREPARATION FOR VICTORIA
GOING ON OUTINGS

* Check bag to ensure that the Days Emergency Drugs Envelope is in the side pocket.

* Collect Rectal Emergency Envelope (VW) (which is kept in fridge) put in side pocket of blue wheelchair bag.

* Pack 6 pads, folding tightly in small white bags . ready for disposal wherever you may be!

* Pack at least 3 changes of trousers/skirts/knickers so that if Victoria has accidents, you have spare clothes.

* Pack 2 empty Shopping plastic bags for wet clothes.

* Pack paper/cards for Victoria to fiddle with. On a long wait, these may prove a life safer for You!

* Pack travel wipes - these can be used not only for face + hands, but also for bottom areas.

* Bags of crisps, Rvita + cheese, small bottle of drink with plastic tooth mug, can be used for emergency rations.

* money, GLC card

* If out for whole day, take something for Victoria to lay down - she will need regular periods of laying down.

* Check bag to ensure Emergency telephone numbers are with you - in case you get stranded! Bon voyage!

This reminds workers of the detailed planning required for a successful outing.

The House Book

When Kathy and Victoria moved into their home, the care agency was very clear that it was usually the user who would direct the worker as to what care was needed and how the household should be run. As both women were unable to do this, the parents had to do it for them. The Operational Policy clearly outlined the duties, but for more detailed instructions and directions we wrote the Care Books to direct the personal care required. The detailed instructions and directions on running the household were eventually brought together in the House Book.

Initially, we thought everyone would know how to work a washing machine or tumble drier, defrost a fridge or follow instructions on how a central heating system operated. However, after a few costly mistakes we found it necessary to provide written instructions that took a worker through the tasks in simple step by step stages. We wrote the instructions on A4 paper, inserted them into plastic sheets, and fixed them on walls near the equipment. But after a short period of time the pages went missing. We also found we had to introduce a system for training the workers in how to do simple things: what to do if the heating went off, or if other repairs or emergencies arose in the house.

The care agency asked the parents, as the women's representatives, to write down everything pertaining to the household. The range was wide, from every domestic chore that was needed, and how it should be done and when; how and when bills should be paid; what to do with any letters addressed to Kathy and Victoria; how to order continence supplies to jobs such as changing a light bulb. Instructions also had to be given for planning hospital visits, outings and shopping. Once the vehicle was acquired, exact details were needed about every aspect of running and maintaining it.

These instructions evolved into the House Book. It is now over fifty pages long in an A4 ring binder with transparent plastic sleeves. We found this the best method for the constant updating that is needed and it is durable enough to be used frequently by many workers. The folder now provides essential instructions, reminders and references for every function and piece of equipment and machinery in the house.

The following pages are self-explanatory.

CONTENTS

CONTENTS

Accidents - Home & Away

Both Lisa, & Victoria can cause & create accidents that you may not fore see.
Again, these are the known ones - add to list!

Victoria   Can reach, pull + poke things that you may think are safe, especially when you go out of the room! Things to watch for her are:-
- Pushing over furniture eg chairs onto people
- Pushing/pulling music centre
- Throwing hard & sharp objects eg Activity Board
- Papers, cups of hot drinks on the table,
- YES she really can reach!

Things People Drop

Accidents have happened when things have been thoughtlessly left around in their reach, + they fiddle and eat things like:-

Felt tip pens, lead pencils
Broken things - beads, bits off plastic
Cigarette Ends
Pebbles
Incontinence Pads
Other people's valuables.

Two workers at all times: See over →

Victoria + Lisa have separate teams. It is essential that each have their own worker at all times.
See   Health & Safety Policy

Two workers at all times continued:

As with anyone using the Special Project scheme, Victoria and Lisa each have a worker assigned to them for specific shifts (except sleep-in duties when one worker is responsible for both women) You must not unless in emergency and with the agreement of management leave either Victoria or Lisa with the other worker eg. pop out for a pint of milk which may seem easier.

Accident

Should an accident occur - check Operational Policy - but of course in the first instance it is the women's safety you must be sure of.

ALARMS IN BEDROOMS

There are alarms in both bedrooms that are plugged into the wall.

These alarms should be used during the night, so that the sleep-in worker can hear if either woman is
- having a fit
- is very distressed

and then can respond to them straight away.

The alarms can also be used during the day, if Lisa and Victoria are 'resting' but 'an ear' needs to be kept on them whilst the worker is elsewhere in the house. i.e. if either of the women were ill.

For instruction booklet, breakdown or repair details — see inside this folder.

BEDS

* Mattresses need to be stripped and aired once a week, e.g. If possible by the window with fresh air and sunlight

* Turn the mattress every week.

* If more sheets etc are needed, tell parents

* Comfridi duvet, pillow and mattress covers are specially coated nylon fabrics.

   To clean: - Simply wipe with damp cloth or if necessary use a little diluted detergent
   - Hand wash using a mild detergent
   - After rinsing, drip dry or cool tumble dry, for a few minutes.

   NEVER PUT IN WASHING MACHINE.

* Victoria's bed. When dressing roll back duvet and use cream coloured spread.

CARPETS

When anything is spilt on any carpet then you must straight away do the following:-

> Using a wet J cloth, with a little washing-up liquid, wipe up the splash.

If this is done immediately, then a stain will not become engrained.

Wheelchair Marks

Sometimes oil/tar marks can be done by stones etc. lodged in the wheelchair wheels. To remove these marks:-

Use 1001 spray, wipe with cloth

Crumbs

Use carpet sweeper immediately

Regular Carpet clean

Needs to be booked by workers with Tony. No charge will be made.

BATH

It is essential to thoroughly clean the bath, using bath cream after every use.

Bath chair – because of the chair's composition it is vital to clean off all Ballium bath oil after every use. If this is not done well, the oil will have an adverse effect on the hoist's chair.

Toilet

Keep Lisa's toilet chair clean. Weekly clean down with disinfectant, but daily wipe –using toilet cloth, after every use.

Toilet seat and basin should also have a weekly wash with disinfectant – but use a separate cloth from Lisa's.

Sink

Regular wash. Ensure that separate soap, nail brush and towel is used for **you** the worker at all times. Staff towels are red, stores of soap are in the sluice room.

BILLS

HOUSE DIARY

Or communication book is used by workers and parents for:

* appointments for both women e.g. doctors, hospitals, dentists etc.

* appointments for people coming to the house - physio, O/T, parents with family & friends, social workers

* A means to remind workers to
  - stay in the house for deliveries, repairs, visits
  - book transport
  - Any arrangements they may have to make
  - order medication for both women
  - Any situation that arises and people should know about e.g. equipment broken, estate news

PERSONAL PINK FOLDERS

These files keep all personal records for both Lisa and Victoria e.g. letters from doctors.

IMPORTANT CARDS ARE KEPT HERE FOR SAFETY

Prescription cards for doctors
Dentist   Exemption Cards
Hospital

BILLS

When a bill arrives at the house, this is what you do :-

1. Date the bill the day it arrived at the house eg. 27.6.93.

2. Telephone Pauline to say the bill is here at the house (In Pauline's absence - Jean)

3. Put the bill in the silver letter rack which is on the table in the lounge.

4. Write in communications book what you have done.

5. Make sure Pauline gets the bill on her weekly visit to the house.

GAS BILLS

Gas Meter

Is situated in the garden, on the wall, left hand side of the dustbin porch.

Gas Bills

Are paid by both women, and come out of their state benefits.

Payment comes from their joint Halifax account, using Jean or Pauline's signature. Actual payment of the bill is done by Jean or Victoria in person at gas showrooms, Upper Street.

Economy

All central heating is gas – so keep individual radiators a heat sensible for Victoria and Lisa's needs. Turn off radiators in rooms not in use, and certainly if you go out.

Close doors to keep in heat.

DO NOT TOUCH THE CENTRAL HEATING CONTROL IN THE KITCHEN. IF you WANT MORE HEAT THEN JUST PRESS THE RED BOOSTER SWITCH – ONCE!

ELECTRICITY BILLS

Electric Meter

Is situated in the garden, on the wall, left hand side of the dustbin porch.

Electricity Bills

Are paid by both women, and come out of their state benefits.

They have a joint account at the Halifax Bldg. Society, Upper Street, whereby a cheque can be withdrawn, using Jean or Pauline's signature. This is usually posted, with the electricity bill by the parents.

Economy

Turn off any lights that are not necessary. Never use the washing machine half-filled with clothes.

Only use tumble dryer to finish off clothes.

Close doors to keep in heat

RENT, WATER, POLL TAX

Rent

The house is a council house, and Lisa and Victoria are the tenants. Both are in receipt of Housing Benefit, so only pay water rates. This payment is a cheque withdrawn from Halifax joint account, and paid quarterly, using their rent card at ... Neighbourhood office.

Poll Tax

Both women are exempt.

Electoral Register

Both women are on the register and are entitled to vote.

Library

Victoria has a library card for Central Library Holloway Road. With your help, she may wish to borrow tapes and books or compact discs. Record in diary date due back to library, so that Victoria returns them in good time.

TELEPHONE

Calls

* ALLS CALLS MADE FROM THE HOUSE must be recorded in the telephone book placed next to the telephone, BY EVERYONE

* Type of Call
a) Relating to Lisa + Victoria, this includes calls made to agency reporting workers not turning up; queries re-shift
b) Personal calls - ONLY TO BE MADE IN AN EMERGENCY

* All calls are itemized and will be checked quarterly by parents and

Bills

See payment of bills

Outer London and International Calls.

Only in an emergency can the women's telephone be used for these calls AND only if permission is sought.
Correct payment, using the bill tariff must be used on these calls are very expensive

Special Service

If you need to know a telephone number - see over

Telephone Repairs cont.

Total Care

An emergency service has been taken out so that repairs are guaranteed to be completed in

4 hours

24 hr, all year round, including Bank holidays.

Details + code no to follow.

But information is already on 837 2098 exchange line as from 11 March 94

TELEPHONE

Out of Order.

Report immediately 152
Tell office
Go out and use call box if necessary.

IT IS ABSOLUTELY ESSENTIAL that the telephone works at all times.

FAULTS

If a fault is outside the House, YOU will have to tell the engineer
1) Key is needed for   Room

2) This room is situated in Kendal House block, right hand side of 95 Kendal Hse. It is on 1st floor + labelled.

3) If engineer does not have key - Shaun (caretaker) 63 Kendal House, has one.

If you are having difficulty it's worth talking to Tara Willson
700 0911 (home)
            work
as she works for British Telecom.

DIARY

Victoria and Lisa each have a personal diary that is an important document that travels with them. It is used to pass on accurate, precise information about both women - to others. It is used by workers to get a picture of what has happened the previous day, week or month.

* Accurate recordings of the following are essential for the welfare of both women's health, and should be done automatically at the end of every shift

  Medication - initial when given, and time

  Hair-wash
  Nails
  Exercises } Tick when done
  Outing
  B/o
  Fits

  - Should be written up in detail on to diary they happen

  Fit chart - Front of diary Tick
  Periods - " "

* General comments should be noted eg. unusual things the women notice, or accomplish; mood indicators;

CORRESPONDENCE

OPEN ALL LETTERS - including those addressed to Mrs + Mrs Davis/Willson.

Appointments   Action

* Hospital, G.P visits etc for   - Diary appointment
  Lisa or Victoria   - Tell parents

* People coming to the house -   - Diary
  electricians, social workers, physio, o/T etc. - Tell parents

Bills
Write date received on top right hand   - Put in
corner
See Bills page

Personal
Letters, invites to parties   - Diary
                                      - Tell parents

Any other Correspondence
Note date received and re-direct as soon -   If in doubt,
as possible.   check with

                                             Office

FIRE

Fire Safeguards

* Close all doors when you go out

* Keep a set of window keys in every bedroom ~ by the window

If you discover a fire

* In the kitchen eg. flames in a pan - wet a tea towel and smother flames.

* Close door if you discover a larger fire in the room.

* Evacuate the building <u>with</u> Victoria and Lisa!

* Dial 999 - ask for Fire Brigade
  → from a phone box or neighbours - do not go back into the house.

DOMESTIC CHORES

Domestic Chores.

As part of the women's care package, all domestic chores are included. See operation policy.

has devised a cleaning rota.

The following should be done on a day about basis.

- Buying of all food + household goods, string.
- Preparation of meals, snacks + drinks.

- Washing-up + clearing away & crockery ett.

- Washing, drying, ironing, repairing + putting away clothes.

- Sweeping, vacuuming, dusting + tidying house.

- Keeping bedrooms tidy.

- Keeping personal items, eg. shoes, combs, wheelchairs clean + in good order.

- Check + tidy all cupboards + shop for replacing items in addition to food shopping.

- Gardening tidy as necessary.

- Clean bathroom, shower room + kitchen, hallway. hallway/weekly.

Spring cleaning, see separate instructions.

HEATING

HEATING

The boiler is normally switched to TIMED on the slider switch
The heating then operates
from   6 - 9 am
        4 - 10 pm

For more heat - push the RED Boost button. This gives about 1 hour temporary turn-on if in a timed off period.

Boiler

For heating the house is situated in the kitchen, on the wall with the door. The boiler thermostat knob is left set to 3. Do not turn on/off any knobs.

Problems

For any real problems or obvious malfunctions, noises - switch off the switch on the wall under the boiler marked BOILER - and then relax

For repairs

Phone or call by person to _____ neighbourhood office, telling them disabled women live in the house.

Temperature Control and Fuel Economy

There are NO room or building thermostats. ALL CONTROL is via the individual radiator thermostat knobs. Generally a setting of 2-3 seems about right. So if you are not using a room eg. bedroom TURN OFF Radiator. If you are out for hours turn off all radiators

LIGHT FITTINGS

The only light fitting that may cause trouble is in the bathroom.

To take off the plastic cover

* feel around the join of the clear plastic and the brown plastic base

* when your fingers feel a small niche (and it is hard to find)

* Insert a screwdriver or small coin and twist

* the cover will then come off.

← base
← small niche
← clear cover

HOT WATER

All water is heated by the boiler, which is constant

Immersion Heater

The switch for this is on the wall by the utility room and should only be used if the central heating is out of action and is awaiting repair.

The Immersion is a back-up system for hot water.

Airing Cupboard

Is situated next to the utility room.

Use the shelf above the hot water tank for airing towels, sheets and bulky jumpers.

Shower - In Bathroom

To operate the shower, pull the cord which switches it on, an orange light will show at base. (See operates shower unit later in book.

BOILER

Situated in the kitchen.

If the boiler cuts out follow these steps

1. Switch off boiler switch, control switch and thermostat.

2. Wait approx 15 mins before re lighting

3. Press reset button (hole on bottom of boiler) by holding in with index finger.

4. Still holding reset button in, switch on boiler switch, control switch and thermostat. You'll know its on by sound and flames visible through small porthole.

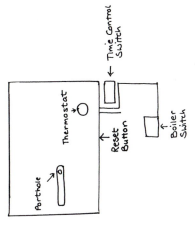

Porthole

Thermostat

Reset Button

← Time Control Switch

← Boiler Switch

INCONTINENCE SUPPLIES

<u>Refer to</u>   Continence Advisor

<u>Pads</u> are delivered monthly from Supplies office
_____

Disposal of Pads

Should be bagged up individually in small white bags, and immediately put into the duster. Bags supplied by Jean or Pauline <u>on request</u>.

Basic Hygiene
Workers should always wash hands with White soap, using nailbrush, if required. Hands should be dried on workers' blue towel, and not the woman's personal towel. This goes some way to stop cross infection.

CANCEL deliveries if boxes of pads builds up. Storing them in the hall is a fire hazard

HOSPITAL VISITS

It is usual for a parent to always accompany their daughter on a hospital visit. However, there may be a rare occasion when they cannot attend, but two workers be arranged for two people to take either Lisa or Victoria.

All hospital visits are important, and are there to attend to the women, and also answer any points relevant to their knowledge of both woman.

Hospital visits need to be planned, so information has to be gathered and equipment/aids in case of a long wait!

So make sure both women eats <u>before</u> appointment.

Checklist
  Hospital card
  Latest details of medication dosage
  Fit charts
  Weight of woman
  Information from team about a particular concern eg unusual behaviour

  Change of Clothes
  Incontinence Pads
  Wet Ones
  China mug, plastic apron
  Food - crisps, small sandwich
  Flask with drink
  Things to amuse!

INSURANCE

A comprehensive insurance policy is paid for by both women.

This covers all contents and all personal belongings
- by forcible/violent theft only
- accidental damage to contents of house

Items that go missing

It is important to immediately tell the parents or if you notice if <u>any</u> item appears to be missing e.g. furniture, crockery, towels, clothes

The rest of the team can then be asked when they last saw the item in question.

If, after a thorough check, we will assume there has been a theft, then the police will automatically be called, either by workers, parents or

An insurance claim will then be submitted. The policy is kept by the parents.

All items are marked with ultra-violet, and a comprehensive list of all household furniture and personal items are kept.

Accidents

If an accident happens, either by a worker or the women (and this does happen!) and equipment is broken/burnt or spoilt, tell immediately, making a note of all details. These can then be possibly claimed by the parents

---

SECURITY

KEYS

There are many keys for this house, and they are EXTREMELY difficult to replace, so please take care of them at all times.

FRONT DOOR/GATE

Victoria :   } Workers must keep these keys on their person at all times
Lisa :
Willsons :
Davis's :
3 Sets : Held at _____

* The set includes a special security lock key to the front door, which can only be re-ordered via Social Services.

BEDROOMS AND LOUNGE

Keys _____ to the _____ are
in _____
Spares are _____

WINDOW LOCK KEYS
- Staff room window key _____
- Lounge window key _____
- For all small upper window lock keys are _____

PARKING SPACE KEYS

Two sets are _____
Jean + Norman - one set
Pauline + Tony - one set

VAN KEYS

Kept in _____ . Spares with parents.

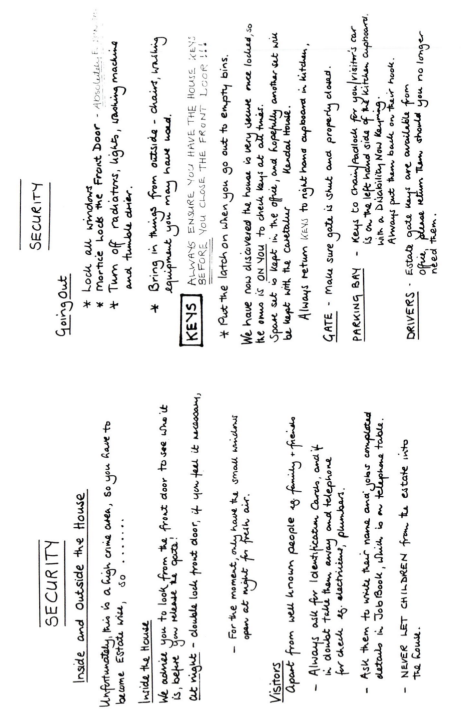

SECURITY

Going Out

* Lock all windows
* Mortice lock the Front Door - Absolutely, F...
* Turn off radiators, lights, washing machine and tumble drier.

* Bring in things from outside - chairs, washing equipment you may have used.

* ALWAYS ENSURE YOU HAVE THE HOUSE KEYS BEFORE YOU CLOSE THE FRONT DOOR !!!

* Put the latch on when you go out to empty bins.

KEYS

We have now discovered the house is very secure once locked, so the onus is ON YOU to check keys at all times.

Spare set is kept in the office, and hopefully another set will be kept with the caretaker Kendal House.

Always return KEYS to right hand cupboard in kitchen.

GATE - Make sure gate is shut and properly closed.

PARKING BAY - Keys to chain/padlock for you/visitor's car is on the left hand side of the kitchen cupboard with a Disability Now keyring. Always put them back on their hook.

DRIVERS - Estate gate keys are available from office; please return them should you no longer need them.

SECURITY

Inside and Outside the House

Unfortunately, this is a high crime area, so you have to become Estate wise, so ....

Inside the House

We advise you to look from the front door to see who it is, before you release the gate!

At night - double lock front door, if you feel it necessary.

- For the moment, only have the small windows open at night for fresh air.

Visitors

Apart from well known people eg family + friends

- Always ask for Identification Cards, and if in doubt take them away and telephone for check eg electricians, plumbers.

- Ask them to write their name and jobs completed details in Job Book, which is on telephone table.

- NEVER LET CHILDREN from the estate into the house.

MACHINES

COOKER

It is essential that this is cleaned after every use, otherwise grease will build up. Use the extractor overhead at times of cooking as this will reduce grease build-up over kitchen as a whole.

FRIDGE/FREEZER

It is essential to keep these machines extremely clean. Thorough washing through the fridge every week. Keep food in covered boxes.
Defrost and clean freezer section once a month
Replace light bulbs in fridge.

VACUUM CLEANER

Change bags when they are full.

Change filter.

NOTE:

Both the fridge and vacuum have a guarantee service. Ask the parents who have the documents. So for ANY REPAIRS ask them in the first instance

LEISURE PASS

Both Lisa and Victoria have passes that admit them, and the people with them

FREE to Islington Leisure Centres & Swimming Pools

The original letter is in clear film, usually kept in their bedroom cupboard or bags. Copy on the reverse of this page.

Leisure Centres
Sobell, Finsbury and Britania offer a whole range of sports activities, as well as massage etc. for women with disabilities.
If you are looking for somewhere to go, just visit one of these centres – they have canteen facilities!

Swimming Pools

Caledonian Road (nearest) –   Both have good
Highbury   access + facilities.

Archway   –   Sat. 10.30 am – 12 noon for disabled people only. Excellent heated pools
Women only Sunday afternoons.

Tumble Drier

1. Switch on at mains, above worktop, to left.

2. Check fluff filter is clean.

3. Select drying time — see front of machine.

4. Press start programme button.

5. When programme is finished, "drying time" slot will show "•".
   Press "door open" button.

Clean fluff filter (at back, inside drier)
Twist anti-clockwise, remove fine mesh screen, remove fluff.

Re-assemble, replace on shaft at back of drum, turning clockwise until locked in position.

MICRO-WAVE

To re-heat a plated meal from the Fridge only not frozen:-

    Press — AUTO RE HEAT MEAL
  and   START Button

Always cover the plate with cling film or another plate.
If not hot enough repeat above.

Jacket Potatoes

An average medium potato takes between 5-15 mins on High.

    Press — Power Button
        " — Amount of time needed
        " — START

An instruction booklet is in the file in the second drawer down-kitchen unit next to cooker.

Washing Machine

1. Check mains supply on; above worktop, to right.
   Sort clothes/linen into groups; see care labels. If in doubt, or if mixed load, use the lower temperature/less vigorous programme.

2. Rinse soiled clothes/linen down sluice.

3. Empty pockets, close zips etc.
   Load machine. (If door closed, put programme selector in "•" position and press "door open" button)

4. Close door, check it latches properly.
   Add powder and conditioner — drawer on left front.

5. pre-wash powder (not all programmes) — conditioner / main wash powder — I, II

   Choose suitable programme from programme guide on front of machine.
   Select programme letter by moving programme selector wheel to a "click".

6. Press programme option buttons if appropriate.

Do not tumble dry

Socks / tights
Gloves / mittens / hats / scarves
Tee-shirts
Track suit tops & bottoms
Sweat shirts
Sweaters, jumpers, cardigans
Clothes with fancy trimmings
Any ITEM with this label: ⊠

Shake and hang these items on the floor-standing airer or overhead airer, to dry.

These items will shrink and/or lose their shape if tumble dried.

MAIN WASH PROGRAMMES

	Programme		Items
95	WHITES HEAVY SOIL	A	Sheets, draw sheets, white cotton pillowslips etc.
95	WHITES	B	As above, if you heavily soiled
60	FAST COLOUREDS	C	towels, face flannels, bibs, table cloths, tea towels, etc
40	NON-FAST COLOUREDS	D	duvet covers, poly-cotton pillow slips, shirts, blouses, vests, dresses, skirts etc.
40	DELICATES	K	track suit tops and bottoms, socks, tights, sweatshirts, most trousers, etc.

N.B. Delicate items:-

	Programme	
40	WOOLLENS	E+ WOOL OPTION
30	COOL WASH	L
	SUPER CARE	E+ WOOL + ECONOM

REPAIRS

Both machines have a 4-year contract for ALL REPAIRS that are FREE.

PHONE: 081 422 7522

Agreement Nos
100 383 0693
100 383 0692

Washing Machine

7. Press start/stop button to start wash. If you select wrong programme, press start/stop button again and select correct programme.

8. When finished, press start/stop button and machine indicator light will go out.
Open door - press "door open" button. (up to 90 second delay after wash has finished)
N.B. door can only be opened when programme selector is in "•" position.

9. Crease guard - some delicate programmes stop on final rinse with drum full of water - press "creaseguard" button and machine will pump out and spin.

10. If something goes wrong, see instruction booklet (above washing machine)

Leave door open between washes - otherwise machine gets smelly.

HOW TO RE-ORDER MEDICATION

All medication is on prescription and both women do not pay.

All medication must be re-ordered by .... workers.

Responsibility rests with Lisa's team and Victoria's team to note when pills, creams, lactories, oils run out.

To ensure they _never_ run out, when a prescription has been renewed, count out number of pills used per day, work out 3 working days _before_ supply runs out and note in their Diaries and House Diary to order another prescription. Check on the day diaried that prescription has been ordered "sign" as ordered.

To re-order:

Give 48 hours notice and using the re-ordering prescription card found in Pink Personal Folder, take this to:-

Dr. _____

Tel: *** ***

Give this card to receptionist and ask for a repeat prescription of what you need for either women.

Chemists

Both women have computer records at _____ Street, NI.   Tel: *** ****

But there is a friendly chemist at ts doesn't end of Copenhagen Street, and its worth building up a friendly relationship.

WASHING POWDER

USE ONLY _PERSIL ORIGINAL_

NON-BIOLOGICAL for the washing machine.

This is really important as Victoria is highly allergic to _any_ other powder _except_

DREFT - for hand washing for woollens etc.

CONDITIONER

Use LENOR or COMFORT

HOUSEHOLD KITTY

Lisa and Victoria will have about £100 of benefits to live on per week. Out of this will have to come all bills - heating, lighting, water, gas, insurance, personal items, leisure + pleasure, and of course food and drink!

£25 each is put every Sunday night by Pauline and Jean into the kitty, which is in the RED TIN - kitchen drawer.

This money should be used for:
- All food
- Drinks - tea, coffee, milk
- Toilet rolls
- Washing up liquid
- Washing powder
- Soap
- Household cleansing materials
- Electric light bulbs
- Black plastic bags

Keep stocked up - Emergency store cupboard
- Long life milk
- Tea, sugar
- Rice
- Pasta
- A tin of Fish, Tomatoes, Beans.

IMPORTANT

All purchases must be recorded in the Household Kitty Cash Book. This is essential, as it provides accountability for team, a guide guideline on how much it costs to live weekly. The money is balanced weekly, at present by Pauline + Jean - in the future by social worker.

PERSONAL MONEY

For personal items, £10 per week is put in by by parents into the tin held in their bedroom cupboard.

This money should be used for: -

* Toiletries - Shampoo
Conditioner
Soap
Toothpaste
Creams
Hairslides etc.

Travel Expenses: - GLC Cab fares
Dial-a-Ride fares

Social/outings - Drinks,
Meals
Admission to swimming/leisure activities
Entertainment

* It is the staff teams responsibility to replenish these items when necessary.

IMPORTANT

A small cash book, kept on top of the tin should be used to note down when items are bought. This is essential, as it provides accountability for team members, and gives guidelines on how much it costs to live independantly.

OUTINGS

* See the map with places of interest in Islington.

* Both Lisa and Victoria like atmosphere, sometimes hustle and bustle, so be adventuresome and visit crowded areas like Kings Cross, Euston stations, Chapel Market - they will be exciting for them.

* The following list is not exhaustive, so please add those you find are interesting for them.

- Covent Garden, includes street entertainers

- Festival Hall & National Theatre in the foyers have free musicians entertaining

- Hackney Empire - have wheelchair access, need to phone first, seats conveniently next to bar!

- Regents Park, Kenwood, Finsbury Park all have inside/outside cafeterias with access.

- Kenwood - Evening summer concerts in open air.

- Trafalgar Square - and surrounding areas.

- Museums, London museum has music & good cafeteria.

MUSIC CENTRE & MUSIC

Music Centre
Was brought from donations to Kathy at the time of her funeral. It is a living memory for a wonderful human being, who loved music. It is donated to the house to bring music and joy into people's lives, and to remember a very special person.

Radio
Has been set automatically - but read book of instructions

Tapes
You can record from one tape to another, so if you have favourite music - introduce it to Victoria. Spare blank tapes in drawer. Run through cleaning tape at the first of every month.

Compact Discs
Need to take out light plug to put compact disc plug in wall socket.
Borrow compact discs and tapes from libraries.

Repairs
Speak in the first instance to parents.
Victoria's Sony has a guarantee for all parts

REPAIRS

Major repairs   when you notice things go wrong

— record this in the House Diary

— report it immediately to   Neighbourhood Office
leaving a clear message for the Estate Manager.
Always tell them that 95 Kendal House is a
home for two disabled women. See over for times.

— On your return to the house, record your visit
to the N. office in diary and White Board in
the hall.

Major repairs would include   Heating, Boiler, toilets
drains, bathroom, shower a structural things to
the house.

Minor Repairs

Bathrails, damage to furniture by Victoria or others,
pictures broken - small things not working properly

* In the first instance tell Norman or Tony.
They are extremely good for small jobs and
will do them as soon as they can.
Its also worth checking out with them about
any problems you have with machinery etc.

* Will all workers keep a running list - see over
so that everyone knows what needs doing
and when it has been done!

RUBBISH

In the House:

Incontinence Pads   should be bagged up immediately
and used in the small white bags, trying top
tightly. These bags are kept in Victoria's shower room
+ Lisa's bedroom.
They should then be put immediately into black bag
outside the house.
Remember - these pads are a HEALTH HAZARD
to everyone !

(Tell Jean when bags are running low)

White Plastic Waste Bins   should not be used for pads,
+ should be emptied daily using bin liners, when required.

Kitchen Bin   - empty daily

Outside the House

Unfortunately the house will not have a dustbin collection
so ....

When a Black Bag is full, tie top tightly and put
in the Silver paladins adjacent to the house. Do not
fill rubbish up to the top of the bags, as this might
prove too heavy for some care officers.
Buy black bags from Chapel market stalls -
they are the cheapest.

SHOWER UNIT

The shower head of the small electric shower in the bathroom should be cleaned out at least once every week.

To do this insert screwdriver or small coin in slot and turn in the direction indicated

Tap shower head on hand till all the bits are out. When cleaned, replace by reversing this process

If shower head is not cleaned the water will run hot.

slot

VICTORIA'S SHOWER

The head of the shower in Victoria's shower room does not need cleaning more than once every six months.

To do this take out centre screw, turn outside chrome ring, the centre will then come out.

When clean, reverse process

At all times keep the shower hose away from Victoria's right hand.

central screw

SHOWER in BATHROOM

How to 'operate the shower:-

1. Switch on - the switch is situated next to light switch, left hand side of bathroom door

2. Switch - is a cord
   pull this cord

3. An orange light will show at the base of the cord, near the ceiling

4. The shower is now switched on

5. Proceed to turn TRITON shower to 'HOT' over the bath.

TRANS PORT

GLC Taxi Card

Lisa's No:
Victoria's No:

Telephone Radio Taxis ** *** to book taxi

Dial-A-Ride

Bookings can only be made hours before journey and only between the hours of

Lisa's No:
Victoria's No: ** ***

Mini Cabs

If taxi cabs fail to arrive, phone for mini cab telling them you have a wheelchair for the boot.

N.L. Cars - _____

PAYING FOR ALL TRANSPORT

Workers will take this out of womens personal money, noting details in book.

SMOKE ALARMS

This is a non-smoking house!

If anyone wishes to smoke, then they should be directed to the garden with an ashtray for butts!

There are 3 smoke alarms:-

- In the hall by the telephone

- In Victoria's bedroom

- In Lisa's bedroom

The smoke alarms have batteries, when these run low they bleep. It is essential for everyone's safety, to replace these batteries as soon as you can

Please remove cigarette butts from garden.

VAN INSTRUCTIONS

THE VAN AXES Q - STAR   PETROL

Sept 97.Instructions for use of vehicle Volkswagon Transporter Reg .

Outside Bungalow;Always park vehicle in own parking bay.Make sure chain if fully across and locked at all times.

Keys;Keys to be kept in cupboard in kitchen with street door keys.Same key that operates vehicle unlocks petrol cap.

Log Book;There is a log book in vehicle to log all journeys,mileage etc.

Private Use; There will be No private use of vehicle, it is solely for Lisa and Victorias use only.

Disabled Badges;These are kept in the glove compartment of vehicle, to be used when parking on meters or single yellow lines.The badges don't allow you to park in or on the following places.Double yellow lines,resident parking bays unless own.south of Euston Road in Camden,Royal Borough of Kensington & Chelsea, Borough of Westminister. Always use timer badge with disabled badge.

Use of Ramp;Always pull out in a straight line till fully extended,then place upon floor of bus,the same applies in reverse for putting ramp away.

Servicing;To be done by Tony on a 4 monthly period.

Breakdowns;AA card in glove compartment,always to be kept there.

Cleaning of vehicle;Inside to be kept clean by staff.Outside parents to arrange.

Petrol,Oil,Water.To be checked weekly by staff.Petrol to be put in by staff on Mondays and Fridays,never let the vehicle run out of petrol. *Never let Petrol go under 1/4 tank YL mark in Petrol gauge*

Budget for vehicle;Both women will pay £7 per week each for petrol.£7 is the equivalent of 770 miles.

Priority Journeys.Hospital visits,doctors appointments,shopping,Organised activities e.g. Shape,Wheelchair dancing,Laundry Club.If Flexi team need to use taxis then worker will drive to and from.

Insurance of vehicle;Any driver over 25 with full,clean-driving UK license.

All workers to be tested a)Vehicle empty.b)Vehicle with Lisa and Victoria as passengers.Reversing,parking,braking,anticipation and checking mirrors,speed.

Security;Nothing to be left in vehicle,deters thieves.Steering lock to be kept on at all times when not in use.Clamps and seat belts at all times.Lisa and Victoria can be taken out without additional escort. *Routeing,* Tony,Tara or Norman to drive. *Pauline*

Schedule of use;Planned activities determine which women has 1st dibs to use,this includes shopping rota. Each week /fortnight workers to draw up outings etc. requiring transport-senior(s) to agree usage.Bottom line budget determines sharing.Wherever possible compromise to be reached.

In the event of an accident;Do not panic. Do not say it was your fault.Make sure passengers and self are alright.Take down other drivers name,address telephone number.Take registration Number and make of car and colour.Ask for witnesses,phone police.If possible drive home,if not ring AA and get tow.Last but not least phone Tony and break the news

PLAN OF THE BUNGALOW

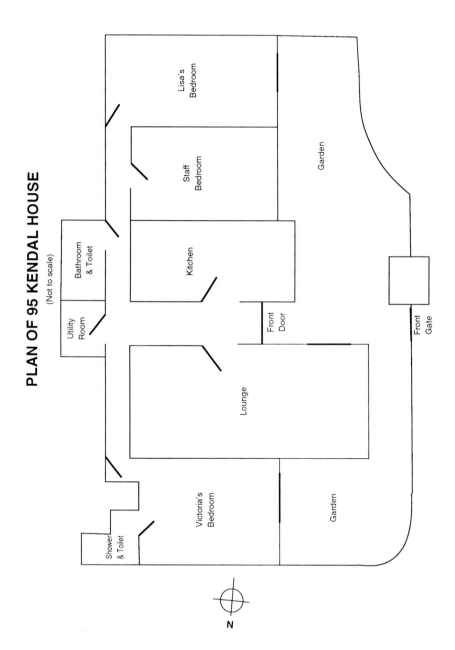

PLAN OF 95 KENDAL HOUSE

(Not to scale)

Lisa's Bedroom

Staff Bedroom

Garden

Bathroom & Toilet

Kitchen

Utility Room

Front Door

Lounge

Front Gate

Victoria's Bedroom

Garden

Shower & Toilet

N

Index